English / Arabic

انجليــزي / عربـــي

THE OXFORD

Picture Dictionary

NORMA SHAPIRO AND JAYME ADELSON-GOLDSTEIN

Translated by Cambridge Translation Resources, Inc.

D1319402

Oxford University Press

Oxford University Press
198 Madison Avenue, New York, NY 10016 USA
Great Clarendon Street, Oxford OX2 6DP England

Oxford New York

Auckland Cape Town Dar es Salaam Hong Kong Karachi
Kuala Lumpur Madrid Melbourne Mexico City Nairobi
New Delhi Shanghai Taipei Toronto
With offices in

Argentina Austria Brazil Chile Czech Republic France Greece
Guatemala Hungary Italy Japan South Korea Poland Portugal
Singapore Switzerland Thailand Turkey Ukraine Vietnam

OXFORD is a trademark of Oxford University Press.

Copyright © 1998 Oxford University Press

ISBN-13: 978-0-19-436197-2
ISBN-10: 0-19-436197-7

Library of Congress Cataloging-in-Publication Data

Shapiro, Norma.
    The Oxford picture dictionary. English-Arabic /
Norma Shapiro and Jayme Adelson-Goldstein; translated by
Cambridge Translation Resources.
         p.   cm.
    Includes bibliographical references (p.   ) and
    indexes.
    ISBN 0-19-436197-7
    1. Picture dictionaries, Arabic.   2. Picture dictionaries,
    English.   3. Arabic language—Dictionaries—English.   4.
    English language—Dictionaries—Arabic.   I. Adelson-
    Goldstein, Jayme.   II. Title.
PJ6640.S485   1998   98-10708
423'.927—dc21

Translation reviewed by: Karam S. Tannous
Editorial Manager: Susan Lanzano
Art Director: Lynn Luchetti
Senior Editor: Eliza Jensen
Senior Designer: Susan P. Brorein
Senior Production Editor: Robyn F. Clemente
Art Buyer: Tracy A. Hammond
Cover Design Production: Brett Sonnenschein
Production Manager: Abram Hall
Production Services by: Cambridge Translation Resources, Inc.
Cover design by Silver Editions

Printing (last digit): 10 9

Printed in China

Illustrations by: David Aikins, Doug Archer, Craig Attebery,
Garin Baker, Sally Bensusen, Eliot Bergman, Mark Bischel, Dan
Brown / Artworks NY, Roy Douglas Buchman, George Burgos /
Larry Dodge, Rob Burman, Carl Cassler, Mary Chandler, Robert
Crawford, Jim DeLapine, Judy Francis, Graphic Chart and Map
Co., Dale Gustafson, Biruta Akerbergs Hansen, Marcia
Hartsock, C.M.I., David Hildebrand, The Ivy League of Artists,
Inc. / Judy Degraffenreid, The Ivy League of Artists, Inc. / Tom
Powers, The Ivy League of Artists, Inc. / John Rice, Pam
Johnson, Ed Kurtzman, Narda Lebo, Scott A. MacNeill /
MACNEILL & MACINTOSH, Andy Lendway / Deborah Wolfe
Ltd., Jeffrey Mangiat, Suzanne Mogensen, Mohammad
Mansoor, Tom Newsom, Melodye Benson Rosales, Stacey
Schuett, Rob Schuster, James Seward, Larry Taugher, Bill
Thomson, Anna Veltfort, Nina Wallace, Wendy Wassink-
Ackison, Michael Wepplo, Don Wieland
Thanks to Mike Mikos for his preliminary architectural sketches
of several pieces.

References
Boyer, Paul S., Clifford E. Clark, Jr., Joseph F. Kett, Thomas L.
Purvis, Harvard Sitkoff, Nancy Woloch *The Enduring Vision: A
History of the American People*, Lexington, Massachusetts:
D.C. Heath and Co., 1990.

Grun, Bernard, *The Timetables of History: A Horizontal Linkage
of People and Events*, (based on Werner Stein's Kulturfahrplan)
New York: A Touchstone Book, Simon and Schuster, 1946,
1963, 1975, 1979.

Statistical Abstract of the United States: 1996, 116th Edition,
Washington, DC: US Bureau of the Census, 1996.

The World Book Encyclopedia, Chicago: World Book Inc., a
Scott Fetzer Co., 1988 Edition.

Toff, Nancy, Editor-in-Chief, *The People of North America*
(Series), New York: Chelsea House Publishers, Main Line
Books, 1988.

Trager, James, *The People's Chronology, A Year-by-Year Record
of Human Events from Prehistory to the Present*, New York:
Henry Holt Reference Book, 1992.

Acknowledgments

The publisher and authors would like to thank the following people for reviewing the manuscript and/or participating in focus groups as the book was being developed:

Ana Maria Aguilera, Lubie Alatriste, Ann Albarelli, Margaret Albers, Sherry Allen, Fiona Armstrong, Ted Auerbach, Steve Austen, Jean Barlow, Sally Bates, Sharon Batson, Myra Baum, Mary Beauparlant, Gretchen Bitterlin, Margrajean Bonilla, Mike Bostwick, Shirley Brod, Lihn Brown, Trish Brys-Overeem, Lynn Bundy, Chris Bunn, Carol Carvel, Leslie Crucil, Jill DeLa Llata, Robert Denheim, Joshua Denk, Kay Devonshire, Thomas Dougherty, Gudrun Draper, Sara Eisen, Lynda Elkins, Ed Ende, Michele Epstein, Beth Fatemi, Andra R. Fawcett, Alice Fiedler, Harriet Fisher, James Fitzgerald, Mary Fitzsimmons, Scott Ford, Barbara Gaines, Elizabeth Garcia Grenados, Maria T. Gerdes, Penny Giacalone, Elliott Glazer, Jill Gluck de la Llata, Javier Gomez, Pura Gonzales, Carole Goodman, Joyce Grabowski, Maggie Grennan, Joanie Griffin, Sally Hansen, Fotini Haritos, Alice Hartley, Fernando Herrera, Ann Hillborn, Mary Hopkins, Lori Howard, Leann Howard, Pamela Howard, Rebecca Hubner, Jan Jarrell, Vicki Johnson, Michele Kagan, Nanette Kafka, Gena Katsaros, Evelyn Kay, Greg Keech, Cliff Ker, Gwen Kerner-Mayer, Marilou Kessler, Patty King, Linda Kiperman, Joyce Klapp, Susan Knutson, Sandy Kobrine, Marinna Kolaitis, Donna Korol, Lorraine Krampe, Karen Kuser, Andrea Lang, Nancy Lebow, Tay Lesley, Gale Lichter, Sandie Linn, Rosario Lorenzano, Louise Louie, Cheryl Lucas, Ronna Magy, Juanita Maltese, Mary Marquardsen, Carmen Marques Rivera, Susan McDowell, Alma McGee, Jerry McLeroy, Kevin McLure, Joan Meier, Patsy Mills, Judy Montague, Vicki Moore, Eneida Morales, Glenn Nadelbach, Elizabeth Neblett, Kathleen Newton, Yvonne Nishio, Afra Nobay, Rosa Elena Ochoa, Jean Owensby, Jim Park, John Perkins, Jane Pers, Laura Peskin, Maria Pick, Percy Pleasant, Selma Porter, Kathy Quinones, Susan Ritter, Martha Robledo, Maureen Rooney, Jean Rose, David Ross, Julietta Ruppert, Lorraine Ruston, Susan Ryan, Frederico Salas, Leslie Salmon, Jim Sandifer, Linda Sasser, Lisa Schreiber, Mary Segovia, Abe Shames, Debra Shaw, Stephanie Shipp, Pat Singh, Mary Sklavos, Donna Stark, Claire Cocoran Stehling, Lynn Sweeden, Joy Tesh, Sue Thompson, Christine Tierney, Laura Topete, Carmen Villanueva, Laura Webber, Renée Weiss, Beth Winningham, Cindy Wislofsky, Judy Wood, Paula Yerman.

A special thanks to Marna Shulberg and the students of the Saticoy Branch of Van Nuys Community Adult School.

We would also like to thank the following individuals and organizations who provided their expertise:

Carl Abato, Alan Goldman, Dr. Larry Falk, Caroll Gray, Henry Haskell, Susan Haskell, Los Angeles Fire Department, Malcolm Loeb, Barbara Lozano, Lorne Dubin, United Farm Workers.

Authors' Acknowledgments

Throughout our careers as English language teachers, we have found inspiration in many places—in the classroom with our remarkable students, at schools, conferences, and workshops with our fellow teachers, and with our colleagues at the ESL Teacher Institute. We are grateful to be part of this international community.

We would like to sincerely thank and acknowledge Eliza Jensen, the project's Senior Editor. Without Eliza, this book would not have been possible. Her indomitable spirit, commitment to clarity, and unwavering advocacy allowed us to realize the book we envisioned.

Creating this dictionary was a collaborative effort and it has been our privilege to work with an exceptionally talented group of individuals who, along with Eliza Jensen, make up the Oxford Picture Dictionary team. We deeply appreciate the contributions of the following people:

Lynn Luchetti, Art Director, whose aesthetic sense and sensibility guided the art direction of this book,

Susan Brorein, Senior Designer, who carefully considered the design of each and every page,

Klaus Jekeli, Production Editor, who pored over both manuscript and art to ensure consistency and accuracy, and

Tracy Hammond, Art Buyer, who skillfully managed thousands of pieces of art and reference material.

We also want to thank Susan Mazer, the talented artist who was by our side for the initial problem-solving and Mary Chandler who also lent her expertise to the project.

We have learned much working with Marjorie Fuchs, Lori Howard, and Renée Weiss, authors of the dictionary's ancillary materials. We thank them for their on-going contributions to the dictionary program.

We must make special mention of Susan Lanzano, Editorial Manager, whose invaluable advice, insights, and queries were an integral part of the writing process.

This book is dedicated to my husband, Neil Reichline, who has encouraged me to take the road less traveled, and to my sons, Eli and Alex, who have allowed me to sit at their baseball games with my yellow notepad. —NS

This book is lovingly dedicated to my husband, Gary and my daughter, Emily Rose, both of whom hugged me tight and let me work into the night. —JAG

A Letter to the Teacher

Welcome to The Oxford Picture Dictionary.

This comprehensive vocabulary resource provides you and your students with over 3,700 words, each defined by engaging art and presented in a meaningful context. *The Oxford Picture Dictionary* enables your students to learn and use English in all aspects of their daily lives. The 140 key topics cover home and family, the workplace, the community, health care, and academic studies. The topics are organized into 12 thematic units that are based on the curriculum of beginning and low-intermediate level English language coursework. The word lists of the dictionary include both single word entries and verb phrases. Many of the prepositions and adjectives are presented in phrases as well, demonstrating the natural use of words in conjunction with one another.

The Oxford Picture Dictionary uses a variety of visual formats, each suited to the topic being represented. Where appropriate, word lists are categorized and pages are divided into sections, allowing you to focus your students' attention on one aspect of a topic at a time.

Within the word lists:

- nouns, adjectives, prepositions, and adverbs are numbered,

- verbs are bolded and identified by letters, and

- targeted prepositions and adjectives within phrases are bolded.

The dictionary includes a variety of exercises and self access tools that will guide your students towards accurate and fluent use of the new words.

- Exercises at the bottom of the pages provide vocabulary development through pattern practice, application of the new language to other topics, and personalization questions.

- An alphabetical index assists students in locating all words and topics in the dictionary.

- A phonetic listing for each word in the index and a pronunciation guide give students the key to accurate pronunciation.

- A verb index of all the verbs presented in the dictionary provides students with information on the present, past, and past participle forms of the verbs.

The Oxford Picture Dictionary is the core of *The Oxford Picture Dictionary Program* which includes a *Dictionary Cassette*, a *Teacher's Book* and its companion *Focused Listening Cassette, Beginning* and *Intermediate Workbooks, Classic Classroom Activities* (a photocopiable activity book), *Overhead Transparencies,* and *Read All About It 1* and *2*. Bilingual editions of *The Oxford Picture Dictionary* are available in Spanish, Chinese, Vietnamese, and many other languages.

TEACHING THE VOCABULARY

Your students' needs and your own teaching philosophy will dictate how you use *The Oxford Picture Dictionary* with your students. The following general guidelines, however, may help you adapt the dictionary's pages to your particular course and students. (For topic-specific, step-by-step guidelines and activities for presenting and practicing the vocabulary on each dictionary page see the *Oxford Picture Dictionary Teacher's Book*.)

Preview the topic

A good way to begin any lesson is to talk with students to determine what they already know about the topic. Some different ways to do this are:

- Ask general questions related to the topic;

- Have students brainstorm a list of words they know from the topic; or

- Ask questions about the picture(s) on the page.

Present the vocabulary

Once you've discovered which words your students already know, you are ready to focus on presenting the words they need. Introducing 10–15 new words in a lesson allows students to really learn the new words. On pages where the word lists are longer, and students are unfamiliar with many of the words, you may wish to introduce the words by categories or sections, or simply choose the words you want in the lesson.

Here are four different presentation techniques. The techniques you choose will depend on the topic being studied and the level of your students.

- Say each new word and describe or define it within the context of the picture.

- Demonstrate verbs or verb sequences for the students, and have volunteers demonstrate the actions as you say them.

- Use Total Physical Response commands to build comprehension of the vocabulary: *Put the pencil on your book. Put it on your notebook. Put it on your desk.*

- Ask a series of questions to build comprehension and give students an opportunity to say the new words:

▶ Begin with *yes/no* questions. *Is #16 chalk?* (yes)

▶ Progress to *or* questions. *Is #16 chalk or a marker?* (chalk)

▶ Finally, ask *Wh* questions.

What can I use to write on this paper? (a marker/ Use a marker.)

Check comprehension

Before moving on to the practice stage, it is helpful to be sure all students understand the target vocabulary. There are many different things you can do to check students' understanding. Here are two activities to try:

• Tell students to open their books and point to the items they hear you say. Call out target vocabulary at random as you walk around the room checking to see if students are pointing to the correct pictures.

• Make true/false statements about the target vocabulary. Have students hold up two fingers for true, three fingers for false. *You can write with a marker.* [two fingers] *You raise your notebook to talk to the teacher.* [three fingers]

Take a moment to review any words with which students are having difficulty before beginning the practice activities.

Practice the vocabulary

Guided practice activities give your students an opportunity to use the new vocabulary in meaningful communication. The exercises at the bottom of the pages are one source of guided practice activities.

• **Talk about...** This activity gives students an opportunity to practice the target vocabulary through sentence substitutions with meaningful topics.

  e.g. **Talk about your feelings.**

    I feel <u>happy</u> when I see my friends.

• **Practice...** This activity gives students practice using the vocabulary within common conversational functions such as making introductions, ordering food, making requests, etc.

  e.g. **Practice asking for things in the dining room.**

    Please pass <u>the platter</u>.

    May I have <u>the creamer</u>?

    Could I have <u>a fork</u>, please?

• **Use the new language.** This activity asks students to brainstorm words within various categories, or may

ask them to apply what they have learned to another topic in the dictionary. For example, on *Colors*, page 12, students are asked to look at *Clothing I*, pages 64–65, and name the colors of the clothing they see.

• **Share your answers.** These questions provide students with an opportunity to expand their use of the target vocabulary in personalized discussion. Students can ask and answer these questions in whole class discussions, pair or group work, or they can write the answers as journal entries.

Further guided and communicative practice can be found in the *Oxford Picture Dictionary Teacher's Book* and in *Classic Classroom Activities*. The *Oxford Picture Dictionary Beginning* and *Intermediate Workbooks* and *Read All About It 1* and *2* provide your students with controlled and communicative reading and writing practice.

We encourage you to adapt the materials to suit the needs of your classes, and we welcome your comments and ideas. Write to us at:

Oxford University Press
ESL Department
198 Madison Avenue
New York, NY 10016

Jayme Adelson-Goldstein

Norma Shapiro

A Letter to the Student

Dear Student of English,

Welcome to *The Oxford Picture Dictionary*. The more than 3,700 words in this book will help you as you study English.

Each page in this dictionary teaches about a specific topic. The topics are grouped together in units. All pages in a unit have the same color and symbol. For example, each page in the Food unit has this symbol:

On each page you will see pictures and words. The pictures have numbers or letters that match the numbers or letters in the word lists. Verbs (action words) are identified by letters and all other words are identified by numbers.

How to find words in this book

- Use the Table of Contents, pages vii–ix.
  Look up the general topic you want to learn about.

- Use the Index, pages 173–205.
  Look up individual words in alphabetical (A–Z) order.

- Go topic by topic.
  Look through the book until you find something that interests you.

How to use the Index

When you look for a word in the index this is what you will see:

the word   the number (or letter) in the word list

apples [ăp/əlz] **50**–4

the pronunciation   the page number

If the word is on one of the maps, pages 122–125, you will find it in the Geographical Index on pages 206–208.

How to use the Verb Guide

When you want to know the past form of a verb or its past participle form, look up the verb in the verb guide. The regular verbs and their spelling changes are listed on pages 170–171. The simple form, past form, and past participle form of irregular verbs are listed on page 172.

Workbooks

There are two workbooks to help you practice the new words:
The Oxford Picture Dictionary Beginning and *Intermediate Workbooks*.

As authors and teachers we both know how difficult English can be (and we're native speakers!). When we wrote this book, we asked teachers and students from the U.S. and other countries for their help and ideas. We hope their ideas and ours will help you. Please write to us with your comments or questions at:

Oxford University Press
ESL Department
198 Madison Avenue
New York, NY 10016

We wish you success!

Jayme Adelson-Goldstein   *Norma Shapiro*

رسالة إلى التلاميذ

تلاميذ اللغة الإنجليزية الأعزاء،

أهلا بكم في قاموس أكسفورد المصور. مجمل الكلمات التي يزيد عددها عن ٣،٧٠٠ كلمة في هذا الكتاب ستساعدكم في دراستكم للغة الإنجليزية.

كما تلاحظون، كل صفحة في هذا القاموس تعلمكم عن موضوع محدد. تم شمل المواضيع في وحدات مستقلة. بحيث أن كافة صفحات كل وحدة هي من نفس اللون ولها نفس الرمز. مثلا، كل صفحة في وحدة الأطعمة يرمز لها بـ :

سترون في كل صفحة صور وكلمات. الصور مشار إليها إما بأرقام أو بحروف مطابقة للأرقام وللحروف في قوائم الكلمات. الأفعال مشار إليها بحروف والكلمات الأخرى مشار إليها بالأرقام.

إيجاد الكلمات في هذا الكتاب

* استعمل جدول المحتويات، صفحة ix-xi.
  راجع الموضوع العام الذي تريد أن تدرسه.
* إستعمل الفهرست، صفحات ١٧٣–٢٠٥.
  راجع الكلمات المستقلة بالترتيب الأبجدي (أ –ي).
* راجع المواضيع واحداً تلو الآخر
  راجع الكتاب حتى تجد الموضوع الذي يثير إهتمامك.

كيف تستعمل الفهرست

عندما تبحث عن كلمة في الفهرست سترى ما يلي:

الرقم (أو الحرف) في قائمة الكلمة	الكلمة
50–4	apples [ăpˈəlz]
رقم الصفحة	اللفظ

اذا كانت الكلمة موجودة على الخريطة، الصفحات ١٢٢–١٢٥، ستجدها في الفهرست الجغرافي على الصفحات ٢٠٦–٢٠٨.

طريقة استعمال دليل الأفعال

عندما تريد معرفة صيغة الماضي لفعل ما أو صيغة أسم المفعول، ابحث عن الفعل في دليل الأفعال. ان الأفعال العادية وتغييراتها الإملائية مدرجة على الصفحات ١٧٠–١٧١. كما ان الصيغة البسيطة وصيغة الماضي وصيغة أسم المفعول للأفعال الغير عادية مدرجة على الصفحة ١٧٢.

دفتر العمل

هناك كراسين للعمل لمساعدتك في التمرن على الكلمات الجديدة:
كراس العمل لقاموس أكسفورد المصور للمبتدئين وكراس العمل للمرحلة المتوسطة.

بصفتنا مؤلفين وأساتذة فإننا ملمّين بصعوبة اللغة الإنجليزية (فهي لغتنا الأصلية). لذلك عندما كتبنا هذا الكتاب طلبنا من الأساتذة والتلاميذ من الولايات المتحدة وغيرها من الدول لمساعدتنا وتقديم ملاحظاتهم. وإننا نأمل أن توفر لكم هذه الأفكار المساعدة في مجال دراستكم. يرجى إرسال تعليقاتكم لنا على العنوان التالي:

Oxford University Press
ESL Department
198 Madison Avenue
New York, NY 10016

نتمنى لكم النجاح والتوفيق!

Jayme Adelson-Goldstein   *Norma Shapiro*

Contents الفهــــرس

Contents الفهـــرس

الفهــرس **Contents**

1. chalkboard
لوح الطباشير

2. screen
شاشة للعرض

3. student
طالب

4. overhead projector
جهاز لعرض «سلايدز»

5. teacher
معلم

6. desk
مكتب

7. chair / seat
مقعد

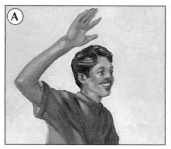

A. Raise your hand.
ارفع يدك.

B. Talk to the teacher.
تحدث إلى المعلم.

C. Listen to a cassette.
استمع إلى شريط.

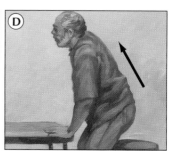

D. Stand up.
قف.

E. Sit down. / Take a seat.
أقعد.

F. Point to the picture.
أشر إلى الصورة.

G. Write on the board.
اكتب/ ي على اللوح.

H. Erase the board.
امسح/ ي اللوح.

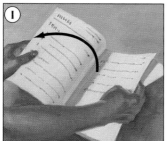

I. Open your book.
أفتح/ ي كتابك.

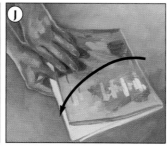

J. Close your book.
أقفل/ ي كتابك.

K. Take out your pencil.
أخرج/ ي قلمك.

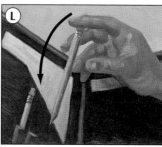

L. Put away your pencil.
أدخل/ ي قلمك.

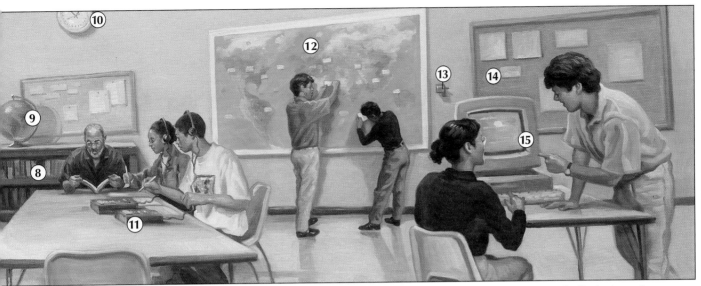

8. bookcase
خزانة كتب

9. globe
كرة أرضية

10. clock
ساعة

11. cassette player
جهاز تسجيل

12. map
خريطة

13. pencil sharpener
مبراة قلم

14. bulletin board
لوحة النشرات

15. computer
كمبيوتر / حاسوب

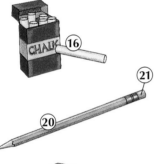

16. chalk
طبشورة

17. chalkboard eraser
ممحاة لوحة الطباشير

18. pen
قلم حبر

19. marker
قلم للتخطيط

20. pencil
قلم رصاص

21. pencil eraser
ممحاة أقلام

22. textbook
الكتاب المدرسي

23. workbook
كراس تمارين

24. binder / notebook
دوسية

25. notebook paper
ورق الدوسية

26. spiral notebook
كراسة بسلك

27. ruler
مسطرة

28. dictionary
قاموس

29. picture dictionary
قاموس مصور

30. the alphabet
حروف الهجاء

31. numbers
أرقام

Use the new language.

1. Name three things you can open.

2. Name three things you can put away.

3. Name three things you can write with.

Share your answers.

1. Do you like to raise your hand?

2. Do you ever listen to cassettes in class?

3. Do you ever write on the board?

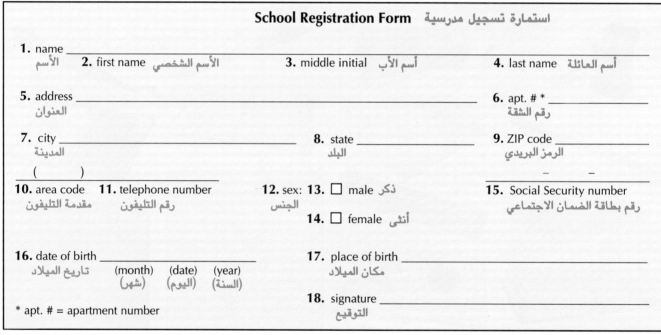

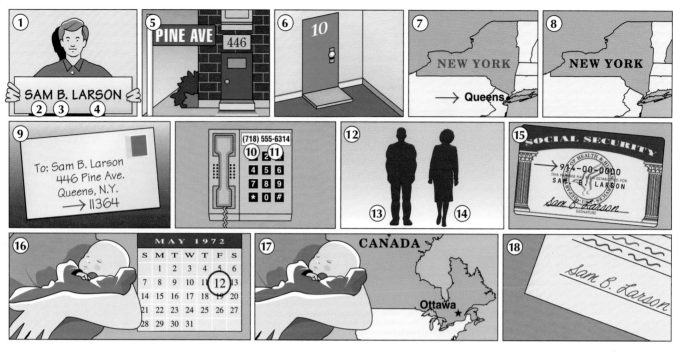

School Registration Form استمارة تسجيل مدرسية

1. name _____
الأسم   **2.** first name   الأسم الشخصي   **3.** middle initial   أسم الأب   **4.** last name   أسم العائلة

5. address _____   **6.** apt. # * _____
العنوان   رقم الشقة

7. city _____   **8.** state _____   **9.** ZIP code _____
المدينة   البلد   الرمز البريدي

(   )   _____ – _____

10. area code   **11.** telephone number   **12.** sex: **13.** ☐ male   ذكر   **15.** Social Security number
مقدمة التليفون   رقم التليفون   الجنس   رقم بطاقة الضمان الاجتماعي
                                                  14. ☐ female   أنثى

16. date of birth _____   **17.** place of birth _____
تاريخ الميلاد   (month) (date) (year)   مكان الميلاد
              (شهر) (اليوم) (السنة)

* apt. # = apartment number   **18.** signature _____
                                      التوقيع

A. Spell your name.
تهجى اسمك.

B. Fill out a form.
املأ الاستمارة.

C. Print your name.
أكتب اسمك بوضوح.

D. Sign your name.
وقع اسمك.

Talk about yourself.

My first name is Sam.

My last name is spelled L-A-R-S-O-N.

I come from Ottawa.

Share your answers.

1. Do you like your first name?

2. Is your last name from your mother? father? husband?

3. What is your middle name?

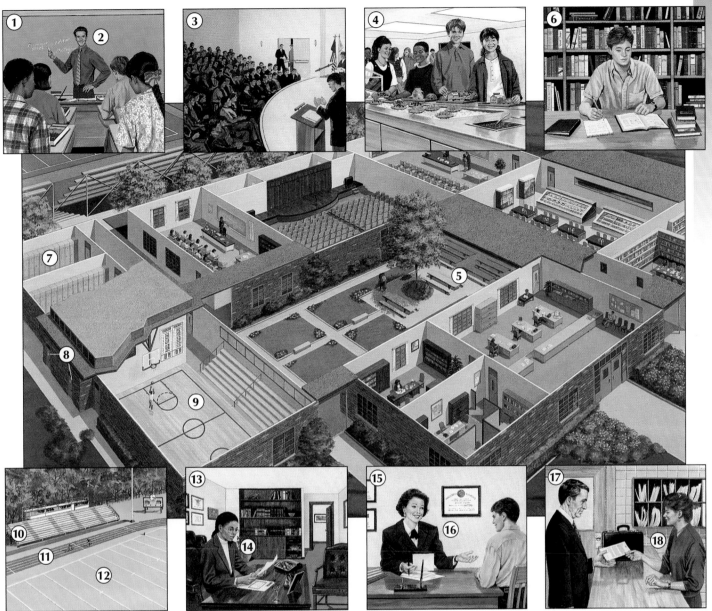

1. classroom
   فصل دراسي / صف
2. teacher
   معلم
3. auditorium
   قاعة
4. cafeteria
   الكافتيريا
5. lunch benches
   مقاعد لتناول وجبة الغذاء
6. library
   مكتبة

7. lockers
   غرفة خلع الملابس
8. rest rooms
   المراحيض
9. gym
   قاعة الرياضة
10. bleachers
    مدرج
11. track
    الحلبة
12. field
    أرض الملعب

13. principal's office
    مكتب مدير المدرسة
14. principal
    المدير
15. counselor's office
    مكتب المشرف
16. counselor
    المشرف
17. main office
    مكتب الإدارة
18. clerk
    موظف / ـة

More vocabulary

instructor: teacher

coach: gym teacher

administrator: principal or other school supervisor

Share your answers.

1. Do you ever talk to the principal of your school?
2. Is there a place for you to eat at your school?
3. Does your school look the same as or different from the one in the picture?

Dictionary work إستخدام القاموس

A. Look up a word.
ابحث عن كلمة.

B. Read the word.
اقرأ الكلمة.

C. Say the word.
أنطق الكلمة.

D. Repeat the word.
أعد الكلمة.

E. Spell the word.
تهجى الكلمة.

F. Copy the word.
انقل الكلمة.

Work with a partner العمل مع زميل

G. Ask a question.
اسأل سؤال.

H. Answer a question.
أجب على سؤال.

I. Share a book.
تعاون بالكتاب.

J. Help your partner.
ساعد زميلك.

Work in a group العمل في مجموعة

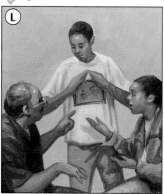

K. Brainstorm a list.
فكر بسرعة لوضع قائمة.

L. Discuss the list.
ناقش القائمة.

M. Draw a picture.
ارسم صورة.

N. Dictate a sentence.
قم بإملاء جملة.

Class work العمل في الفصل/ الصف

O. Pass out the papers.

مرر الأوراق.

P. Talk with each other.

تحدثوا مع بعضكم البعض.

Q. Collect the papers.

اجمع الأوراق.

Follow directions اتبع التعليمات

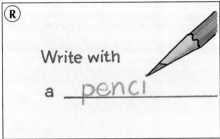

Write with

a _penci_

R. Fill in the blank.

املأ الفراغ

Sign your name in

pen.

pencil.

S. Circle the answer.

ضع علامة حول الإجابة

52 [A] [B] [C] [D] [E]
53 [A] [B] [C] [D] [E]
54 [A] [B] [C] [D] [E]
55 [A] [B] [C]
56 [A] [B] [C] [E]
57 [A] [B] [C] [D] [E]
58 [A] [B] [C] [D] [E]
59 [A] [B] [C] [D] [E]

T. Mark the answer sheet.

علّم الاجابة الصحيحة

pen
pencil
~~desk~~
chalk
marker

U. Cross out the word.

اشطب الكلمة.

Give me the pencil.

V. Underline the word.

ضع خط تحت الكلمة.

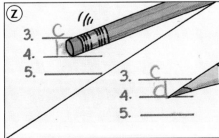

my is pencil. That

That is my pencil

W. Put the words **in order.**

ضع الكلمات في الترتيب الصحيح.

1. sit ___a. pencil
2. write ___b. book
3. read ___c. chair

X. Match the items.

أوصل الكلمات.

1. Draw a ___ pictur
2. Sign with a ___ pen
3. Write with a ___ pen
Discuss a ___
Work wit ___

pen
pencil
pictur

Y. Check your work.

راجع عملك.

3. c
4.
5. ___

3. c
4. d
5. ___

Z. Correct the mistake.

صحّح الأخطاء.

Share your answers.

1. Do you like to work in groups?
2. Do you like to share books?
3. Do you like to answer questions?
4. Is it easy for you to talk with your classmates?
5. Do you always check your work?
6. Do you cross out your mistakes or erase them?

A. greet someone
قم بتحية شخص

B. begin a conversation
ابدأ الحديث

C. end the conversation
إنهي الحديث

D. introduce yourself
عرّف نفسك

E. make sure you **understand**
تأكد من فهمك للحديث

F. introduce your friend
عرّف صديقك

G. compliment your friend
جامل صديقك

H. thank your friend
أشكر صديقك

I. apologize
اعتذر

Practice introductions.

Hi, I'm <u>Sam Jones</u> and this is my friend, <u>Pat Green</u>.

Nice to meet you. I'm <u>Tomas Garcia</u>.

Practice giving compliments.

That's a great <u>sweater</u>, <u>Tomas</u>.

Thanks <u>Pat</u>. I like your <u>shoes</u>.

Look at **Clothing I,** pages **64–65** for more ideas.

 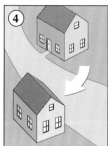  

 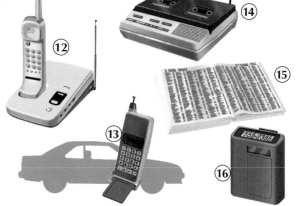 

1. telephone/phone
   جهاز التليفون/الهاتف
2. receiver
   سماعة التليفون/الهاتف
3. cord
   سلك التليفون/الهاتف
4. local call
   مكالمة محلية
5. long-distance call
   مكالمة داخل البلد
6. international call
   مكالمة دولية
7. operator
   البدالة/السنترال
8. directory assistance (411)
   الاستعلامات
9. emergency service (911)
   الطوارئ
10. phone card
    كارت تليفون
11. pay phone
    تليفون عام
12. cordless phone
    تليفون نقال
13. cellular phone
    تليفون خلوي
14. answering machine
    جهاز آلي للرد على المكالمات التليفونية
15. telephone book
    دليل التليفون
16. pager
    جهاز الاستدعاء

Using a pay phone   استعمال تليفون للعموم

A. **Pick up** the receiver.
   ارفع سماعة التليفون.
B. **Listen** for the dial tone.
   استمع إلى صوت اللا إنشغال.
C. **Deposit** coins.
   ضع العملة.

D. **Dial** the number.
   اطلب الرقم.
E. **Leave** a message.
   اترك رسالة.
F. **Hang up** the receiver.
   أغلق سماعة التليفون.

More vocabulary

When you get a person or place that you didn't want to call, we say you have the **wrong number.**

Share your answers.

1. What kinds of calls do you make?
2. How much does it cost to call your country?
3. Do you like to talk on the telephone?

Temperature
درجة الحرارة

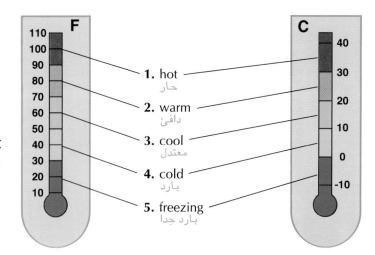

Degrees Fahrenheit
درجة فهرنهايت

Degrees Celsius
درجة مئوية

1. hot
حار
2. warm
دافئ
3. cool
معتدل
4. cold
بارد
5. freezing
بارد جدا

6. sunny/clear
مشمس/صافي

7. cloudy
غائم

8. raining
ممطر

9. snowing
يتساقط الثلج

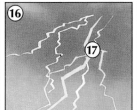   

10. windy
عاصف

11. foggy
ضبابي

12. humid
رطب

13. icy
جليدي

14. smoggy
جو ضبابي ملوث

15. heat wave
موجة حرارية

16. thunderstorm
عاصفة رعدية

17. lightning
برق

18. hailstorm
عاصفة برد

19. hail
برد

20. snowstorm
عاصفة ثلجية

21. dust storm
عاصفة رملية

Language note: *it is, there is*

For **1–14** we use,   *It's <u>cloudy</u>.*

For **15–21** we use,   *There's <u>a heat wave</u>.*
                        There's <u>lightning</u>.

Talk about the weather.

Today it's <u>hot</u>. It's <u>98 degrees</u>.

Yesterday it was <u>warm</u>. It was <u>85 degrees</u>.

1. **little** hand
يد صغيرة
2. **big** hand
يد كبيرة

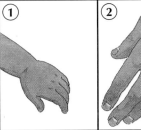

3. **fast** driver
سائق مسرع
4. **slow** driver
سائق بطئ

5. **hard** chair
مقعد قاسي
6. **soft** chair
مقعد مريح

7. **thick** book/
fat book
كتاب سميك/غليظ
8. **thin** book
كتاب رقيق

9. **full** glass
كوب ممتلئ
10. **empty** glass
كوب فارغ

11. **noisy** children/
loud children
أطفال أشقياء/صاخبون
12. **quiet** children
أطفال هادئون

13. **heavy** box
صندوق ثقيل
14. **light** box
صندوق خفيف

15. **neat** closet
دولاب منظم
16. **messy** closet
دولاب غير منظم

17. **good** dog
كلب مطيع
18. **bad** dog
كلب غير مطيع

19. **expensive** ring
خاتم غالي
20. **cheap** ring
خاتم رخيص

21. **beautiful** view
منظر جميل
22. **ugly** view
منظر قبيح

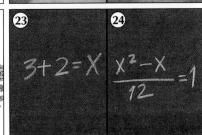

23. **easy** problem
مسألة سهلة
24. **difficult** problem/
hard problem
مسألة صعبة

Use the new language.
1. Name three things that are thick.
2. Name three things that are soft.
3. Name three things that are heavy.

Share your answers.
1. Are you a slow driver or a fast driver?
2. Do you have a neat closet or a messy closet?
3. Do you like loud or quiet parties?

Colors الألـــوان

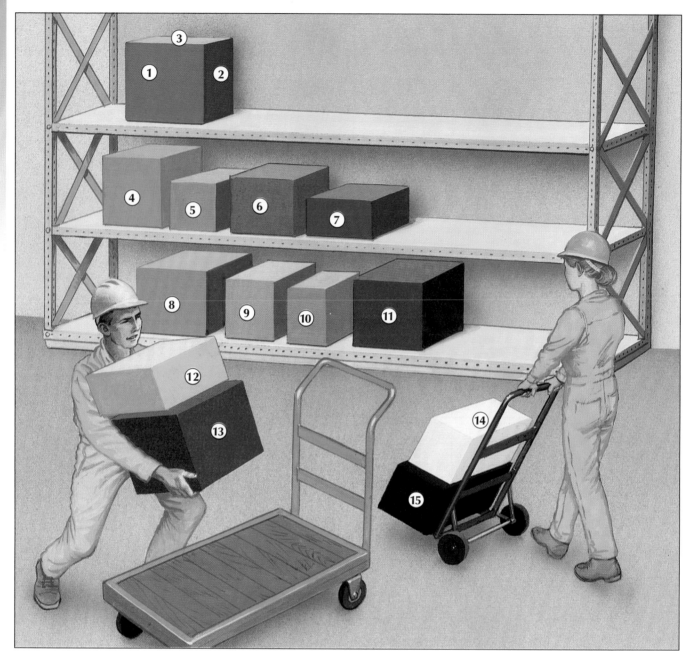

1. blue أزرق	**6.** orange برتقالي	**11.** brown بني
2. dark blue أزرق غامق	**7.** purple بنفسجي	**12.** yellow أصفر
3. light blue ازرق فاتح	**8.** green أخضر	**13.** red أحمر
4. turquoise تركواز/ فيروزي	**9.** beige بيج	**14.** white أبيض
5. gray رمادي	**10.** pink وردي	**15.** black أسود

Use the new language.

Look at **Clothing I,** pages **64–65.**

Name the colors of the clothing you see.

That's a dark blue suit.

Share your answers.

1. What colors are you wearing today?

2. What colors do you like?

3. Is there a color you don't like? What is it?

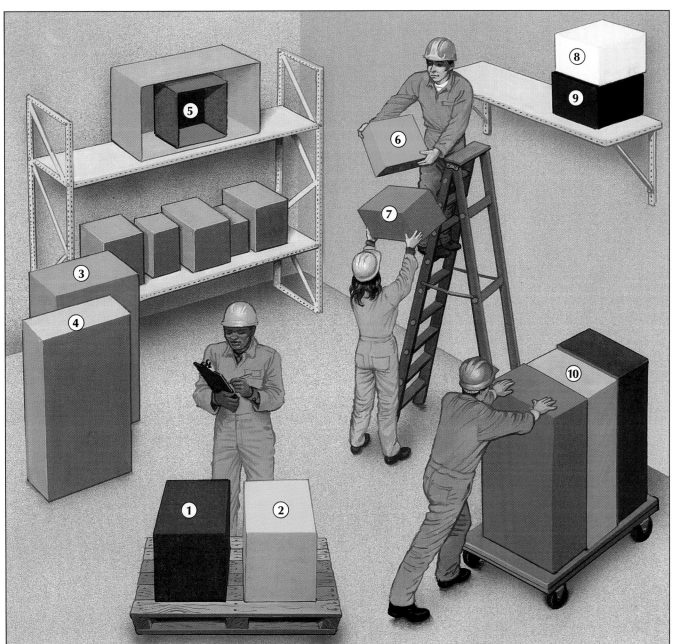

1. The red box is **next to** the yellow box, **on the left.**
   الصندوق الأحمر بجانب الصندوق الأصفر على الجهة اليسرى.
2. The yellow box is **next to** the red box, **on the right.**
   الصندوق الأصفر بجانب الصندوق الأحمر على الجهة اليمنى.
3. The turquoise box is **behind** the gray box.
   الصندوق التركوازي خلف الصندوق الرمادي.
4. The gray box is **in front of** the turquoise box.
   الصندوق الرمادي أمام الصندوق التركوازي.
5. The dark blue box is **in** the beige box.
   الصندوق الأزرق الغامق داخل الصندوق الرمادي.

6. The green box is **above** the orange box.
   الصندوق الأخضر فوق الصندوق البرتقالي.
7. The orange box is **below** the green box.
   الصندوق البرتقالي تحت الصندوق الأخضر.
8. The white box is **on** the black box.
   الصندوق الأبيض على الصندوق الأسود.
9. The black box is **under** the white box.
   الصندوق الأسود تحت الصندوق الأبيض.
10. The pink box is **between** the purple box and the brown box.
    الصندوق الوردي بين الصندوق البنفسجي والصندوق البني.

More vocabulary

near: in the same area
*The white box is **near** the black box.*

far from: not near
*The red box is **far from** the black box.*

HOME	1 8
VISITOR	2 2

SAN DIEGO
235 miles

Cardinals الأعداد الأصلية

0 zero صفر	11 eleven إحدى عشر	21 twenty-one واحد وعشرون	101 one hundred one مائة وواحد
1 one واحد	12 twelve اثنا عشر	22 twenty-two اثنان وعشرون	1,000 one thousand ألف
2 two اثنين	13 thirteen ثلاثة عشر	30 thirty ثلاثون	1,001 one thousand one ألف وواحد
3 three ثلاثة	14 fourteen أربعة عشر	40 forty أربعون	10,000 ten thousand عشرة آلاف
4 four أربعة	15 fifteen خمسة عشر	50 fifty خمسون	100,000 one hundred thousand مائة ألف
5 five خمسة	16 sixteen ستة عشر	60 sixty ستون	1,000,000 one million مليون
6 six ستة	17 seventeen سبعة عشر	70 seventy سبعون	1,000,000,000 one billion بليون
7 seven سبعة	18 eighteen ثمانية عشر	80 eighty ثمانون	
8 eight ثمانية	19 nineteen تسعة عشر	90 ninety تسعون	
9 nine تسعة	20 twenty عشرون	100 one hundred مائة	
10 ten عشرة			

Ordinals الأعداد الترتيبية

1st first الأول	8th eighth الثامن	15th fifteenth الخامس عشر
2nd second الثاني	9th ninth التاسع	16th sixteenth السادس عشر
3rd third الثالث	10th tenth العاشر	17th seventeenth السابع عشر
4th fourth الرابع	11th eleventh الحادي عشر	18th eighteenth الثامن عشر
5th fifth الخامس	12th twelfth الثاني عشر	19th nineteenth التاسع عشر
6th sixth السادس	13th thirteenth الثالث عشر	20th twentieth العشرون
7th seventh السابع	14th fourteenth الرابع عشر	

Roman numerals الأرقام الرومانية

I	= 1	VII	= 7	XXX	= 30
II	= 2	VIII	= 8	XL	= 40
III	= 3	IX	= 9	L	= 50
IV	= 4	X	= 10	C	= 100
V	= 5	XV	= 15	D	= 500
VI	= 6	XX	= 20	M	= 1,000

Fractions الكسور

1. 1/8   one-eighth
ثمن

2. 1/4   one-fourth
رُبع

3. 1/3   one-third
ثلث

4. 1/2   one-half
نصف

5. 3/4   three-fourths
ثلاثة ارباع

6. 1   whole
كامل

1 cup
3/4
2/3
1/2
1/3
1/4

Percents النسب

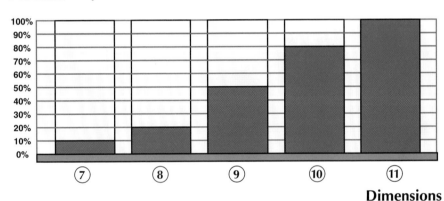

7. 10%   ten percent
عشرة في المائة

8. 20%   twenty percent
عشرون في المائة

9. 50%   fifty percent
خمسون في المائة

10. 80%   eighty percent
ثمانون في المائة

11. 100%   one hundred percent
مائة في المائة

Measurement القياسات

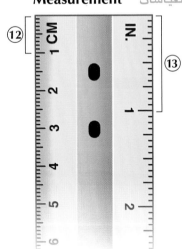

12. centimeter [cm]
سنتيمتر (سم)

13. inch [in.]
بوصة/الإنش

Equivalencies مقاييس متكافئة

1 inch = 2.54 centimeters
1 yard = .91 meters
1 mile = 1.6 kilometers

12 inches = 1 foot
3 feet   = 1 yard
1,760 yards = 1 mile

Dimensions الأبعـــاد

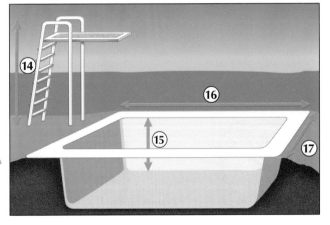

14. height
الارتفاع

15. depth
عمق

16. length
الطول

17. width
العرض

More vocabulary

measure: to find the size or amount of something

count: to find the total number of something

Share your answers.

1. How many students are in class today?

2. Who was the first person in class today?

3. How far is it from your home to your school?

Time الوقت

1. second
ثانية

2. minute
دقيقة

3. hour
ساعة

A.M.
صباحاً

P.M.
مساءً

4. 1:00
one o'clock
الساعة الواحدة

5. 1:05
one-oh-five
five after one
الواحدة وخمسة دقائق

6. 1:10
one-ten
ten after one
الواحدة وعشرة دقائق

7. 1:15
one-fifteen
a quarter after one
الواحدة والربع

8. 1:20
one-twenty
twenty after one
الواحدة وعشرون دقيقة

9. 1:25
one twenty-five
twenty-five after one
الواحدة وخمسة وعشرون دقيقة

10. 1:30
one-thirty
half past one
الواحدة والنصف

11. 1:35
one thirty-five
twenty-five to two
الواحدة والنصف وخمسة دقائق/
الواحدة وخمسة وثلاثون دقيقة

12. 1:40
one-forty
twenty to two
الواحدة وأربعون دقيقة/
الثانية إلا عشرون دقيقة

13. 1:45
one forty-five
a quarter to two
الواحدة وخمسة وأربعون دقيقة/
الثانية إلا ربع

14. 1:50
one-fifty
ten to two
الواحدة وخمسون دقيقة/
الثانية إلا عشرة دقائق

15. 1:55
one fifty-five
five to two
الواحدة وخمسة وخمسون دقيقة/
الثانية إلا خمسة دقائق

Talk about the time.

What time is it? It's 10:00 a.m.

What time do you wake up on weekdays? At 6:30 a.m.

What time do you wake up on weekends? At 9:30 a.m.

Share your answers.

1. How many hours a day do you study English?

2. You are meeting friends at 1:00. How long will you wait for them if they are late?

16

16. morning
صباحاً

17. noon
ظهراً

18. afternoon
بعد الظهر

19. evening
مساءً

20. night
ليلاً

21. midnight
منتصف الليل

22. early
مبكراً

23. late
متأخراً

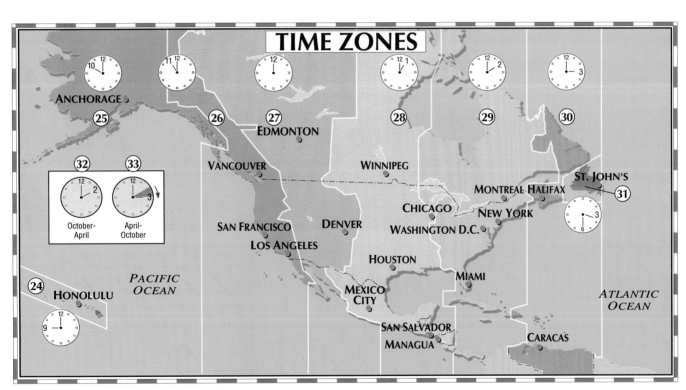

24. Hawaii-Aleutian time
توقيت هاواي – الوشيان

25. Alaska time
توقيت آلاسكا

26. Pacific time
التوقيت الباسيفيكي

27. mountain time
التوقيت الجبلي

28. central time
توقيت الولايات الوسطى

29. eastern time
توقيت الولايات الشرقية

30. Atlantic time
التوقيت الأطلنطي

31. Newfoundland time
توقيت نيو فاوندلاند

32. standard time
التوقيت الشتوي

33. daylight saving time
التوقيت الصيفي

More vocabulary

on time: not early and not late
He's on time.

Share your answers.

1. When do you watch television? study? do housework?

2. Do you come to class on time? early? late?

Days of the week
أيام الأسبوع

1. Sunday
   الأحد
2. Monday
   الأثنين
3. Tuesday
   الثلاثاء
4. Wednesday
   الأربعاء
5. Thursday
   الخميس
6. Friday
   الجمعة
7. Saturday
   السبت
8. year
   سنة
9. month
   شهر
10. day
    يوم
11. week
    أسبوع
12. weekdays
    أيام الأسبوع
13. weekend
    عطلة آخر الأسبوع
14. date
    التاريخ
15. today
    اليوم
16. tomorrow
    غداً
17. yesterday
    أمس
18. last week
    الأسبوع الماضي
19. this week
    الأسبوع الحالي
20. next week
    الأسبوع القادم
21. every day
    كل يوم
22. once a week
    مرة في الأسبوع
23. twice a week
    مرتين في الأسبوع
24. three times a week
    ثلاث مرات في الأسبوع

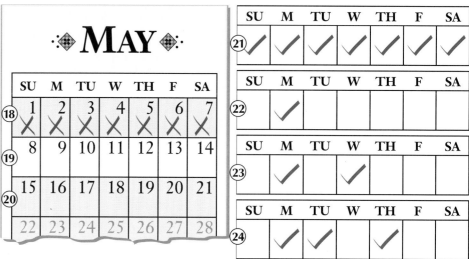

Talk about the calendar.

What's today's date? It's <u>March 10th</u>.

What day is it? It's <u>Tuesday</u>.

What day was yesterday? It was <u>Monday</u>.

Share your answers.

1. How often do you come to school?
2. How long have you been in this school?

2001

JAN (25)
SUN	MON	TUE	WED	THU	FRI	SAT
	1	2	3	4	5	6
7	8	9	10	11	12	13
14	15	16	17	18	19	20
21	22	23	24	25	26	27
28	29	30	31			

FEB (26)
SUN	MON	TUE	WED	THU	FRI	SAT
				1	2	3
4	5	6	7	8	9	10
11	12	13	14	15	16	17
18	19	20	21	22	23	24
25	26	27	28			

MAR (27)
SUN	MON	TUE	WED	THU	FRI	SAT
				1	2	3
4	5	6	7	8	9	10
11	12	13	14	15	16	17
18	19	20	21	22	23	24
25	26	27	28	29	30	31

APR (28)
SUN	MON	TUE	WED	THU	FRI	SAT
1	2	3	4	5	6	7
8	9	10	11	12	13	14
15	16	17	18	19	20	21
22	23	24	25	26	27	28
29	30					

MAY (29)
SUN	MON	TUE	WED	THU	FRI	SAT
		1	2	3	4	5
6	7	8	9	10	11	12
13	14	15	16	17	18	19
20	21	22	23	24	25	26
27	28	29	30	31		

JUN (30)
SUN	MON	TUE	WED	THU	FRI	SAT
					1	2
3	4	5	6	7	8	9
10	11	12	13	14	15	16
17	18	19	20	21	22	23
24	25	26	27	28	29	30

JUL (31)
SUN	MON	TUE	WED	THU	FRI	SAT
1	2	3	4	5	6	7
8	9	10	11	12	13	14
15	16	17	18	19	20	21
22	23	24	25	26	27	28
29	30	31				

AUG (32)
SUN	MON	TUE	WED	THU	FRI	SAT
			1	2	3	4
5	6	7	8	9	10	11
12	13	14	15	16	17	18
19	20	21	22	23	24	25
26	27	28	29	30	31	

SEP (33)
SUN	MON	TUE	WED	THU	FRI	SAT
						1
2	3	4	5	6	7	8
9	10	11	12	13	14	15
16	17	18	19	20	21	22
23/30	24	25	26	27	28	29

OCT (34)
SUN	MON	TUE	WED	THU	FRI	SAT
	1	2	3	4	5	6
7	8	9	10	11	12	13
14	15	16	17	18	19	20
21	22	23	24	25	26	27
28	29	30	31			

NOV (35)
SUN	MON	TUE	WED	THU	FRI	SAT
				1	2	3
4	5	6	7	8	9	10
11	12	13	14	15	16	17
18	19	20	21	22	23	24
25	26	27	28	29	30	

DEC (36)
SUN	MON	TUE	WED	THU	FRI	SAT
						1
2	3	4	5	6	7	8
9	10	11	12	13	14	15
16	17	18	19	20	21	22
23/30	24/31	25	26	27	28	29

MARCH 21 (37)

JUNE 21 (38)

SEPT. 21 (39)

DEC. 21 (40)

JUNE 5 — TIM! (41)

MARCH 2 — ANNIVERSARY (42)

JULY 4 — INDEPENDENCE DAY — STATE BANK — CLOSED - JULY 4 (43)

APRIL 4 — EASTER SUNDAY (44)

MAY 17 — DOCTOR 4:30 (45)

AUGUST (46)

Months of the year
أشهر السنة

25. January
يناير / كانون الثاني

26. February
فبراير / شباط

27. March
مارس / آذار

28. April
ابريل / نيسان

29. May
مايو / أيار

30. June
يونيو / حزيران

31. July
يولو / تموز

32. August
أغسطس / آب

33. September
سبتمبر / أيلول

34. October
أكتوبر / تشرين الأول

35. November
نوفمبر / تشرين الثاني

36. December
ديسمبر / كانون الأول

Seasons
المواسم

37. spring
الربيع

38. summer
الصيف

39. fall
الخريف

40. winter
الشتاء

41. birthday
عيد ميلاد

42. anniversary
ذكرى سنوية

43. legal holiday
عيد رسمي

44. religious holiday
عيد ديني

45. appointment
موعد

46. vacation
عطلة

Use the new language.
Look at the **ordinal numbers** on page **14**.
Use ordinal numbers to say the date.
It's June 5th. It's the fifth.

Talk about your birthday.
My birthday is in the winter.
My birthday is in January.
My birthday is on January twenty-sixth.

Money العملة

Coins نقود معدنية

1. \$.01 = 1¢
a penny / 1 cent
سنت

2. \$.05 = 5¢
a nickel / 5 cents
خمس سنتات

3. \$.10 = 10¢
a dime / 10 cents
عشر سنتات

4. \$.25 = 25¢
a quarter / 25 cents
ربع دولار

5. \$.50 = 50¢
a half dollar
نصف دولار

6. \$1.00
a silver dollar
دولار فضي

Bills عملة ورقية

7. \$1.00
a dollar
دولار

8. \$5.00
five dollars
خمسة دولارات

9. \$10.00
ten dollars
عشرة دولارات

10. \$20.00
twenty dollars
عشرون دولار

11. \$50.00
fifty dollars
خمسون دولار

12. \$100.00
one hundred dollars
مائة دولار

Ways to pay طرق الدفع

13. cash
نقداً

14. personal check
شيك

15. credit card
بطاقة إئتمان

16. money order
حوالة بريدية

17. traveler's check
شيك سياحي

More vocabulary

borrow: to get money from someone and return it later

lend: to give money to someone and get it back later

pay back: to return the money that you borrowed

Other ways to talk about money:

a dollar bill or *a one*

a five-dollar bill or *a five*

a ten-dollar bill or *a ten*

a twenty-dollar bill or *a twenty*

A. shop for
تتسوق

B. sell
تبيع

C. pay for / **buy**
تدفع / تشتري

D. give
تعطي

E. keep
تحتفظ

F. return
ترجع

G. exchange
تستبدل

1. price tag
بطاقة السعر

2. regular price
السعر العادي

3. sale price
السعر المنخفض

4. bar code
شفرة القضبان

5. receipt
الوصل

6. price / cost
السعر / التكلفة

7. sales tax
ضريبة مبيعات

8. total
الاجمالي

9. change
فكة / صرافة

More vocabulary

When you use a credit card to shop, you get a **bill** in the mail. Bills list, in writing, the items you bought and the total you have to pay.

Share your answers.

1. Name three things you pay for every month.

2. Name one thing you will buy this week.

3. Where do you like to shop?

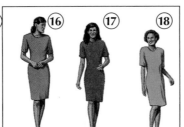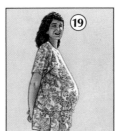

1. children أولاد	**4.** 6-year-old boy طفل عمره ٦ سنوات	**7.** 13-year-old boy ولد عمره ١٣ سنة	**10.** woman إمرأة
2. baby رضيع	**5.** 10-year-old girl طفلة عمرها ١٠ سنوات	**8.** 19-year-old girl بنت عمرها ١٩ سنة	**11.** man رجل
3. toddler طفل	**6.** teenagers مراهقين	**9.** adults بالغ/ راشد	**12.** senior citizen كهل

13. young صغير/ ـة	**17.** average height متوسط/ ـة الطول	**21.** average weight متوسط/ ـة في الوزن	**25.** physically challenged عاجز/ ـة
14. middle-aged متوسط/ ـة العمر	**18.** short قصير/ ـة	**22.** thin/slim نحيف/ نحيفة	**26.** sight impaired/blind ضرير/ ـة
15. elderly عجوز/ ـة	**19.** pregnant حامل	**23.** attractive وسيم/ ـة	**27.** hearing impaired/deaf أصم/ صماء
16. tall طويل/ ـة	**20.** heavyset بدين / بدينة	**24.** cute جميل/ جميلة	

Talk about yourself and your teacher.

I am <u>young</u>, <u>average height</u>, and <u>average weight</u>.

My teacher is <u>a middle-aged</u>, <u>tall</u>, <u>thin</u> man.

Use the new language.

Turn to **Hobbies and Games,** pages 162–163.

Describe each person on the page.

He's <u>a heavyset</u>, <u>short</u>, <u>senior citizen</u>.

Trends Hair Salon
NO APPT. NECESSARY
SHAMPOO
BLOW DRY
CUT

 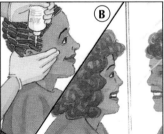  

1. short hair
شعر قصير

2. shoulder-length hair
شعر على الكتف

3. long hair
شعر طويل

4. part
فرق الشعر

5. mustache
شارب

6. beard
لحية

7. sideburns
السبلة الخدية (سوالف)

8. bangs
خصلة

9. straight hair
شعر ناعم

10. wavy hair
شعر مموج

11. curly hair
شعر مجعد

12. bald
أصلع

13. gray hair
شعر شائب

14. red hair
شعر أحمر

15. black hair
شعر أسود

16. blond hair
شعر أشقر

17. brown hair
شعر بني

18. brush
فرشاة

19. scissors
مقص

20. blow dryer
مجفف شعر

21. rollers
بكرة شعر

22. comb
مشط

A. **cut** hair
يقص الشعر

B. **perm** hair
يجعد الشعر

C. **set** hair
يصفّف الشعر

D. **color** hair/**dye** hair
يصبغ الشعر (يلون الشعر)

More vocabulary

hair stylist: a person who cuts, sets, and perms hair

hair salon: the place where a hair stylist works

Talk about your hair.

My hair is <u>long</u>, <u>straight</u>, and <u>brown</u>.

I have <u>long</u>, <u>straight</u>, <u>brown</u> hair.

When I was a child my hair was <u>short</u>, <u>curly</u>, and <u>blond</u>.

23

Tom Lee's Family

1. grandparents
الجدين

Min

Lu

2. grandmother
الجدة

3. grandfather
الجد

4. parents
الوالدين

Rose

Chang

Helen

Daniel

5. mother
الأم

6. father
الأب

10. aunt
العم/الخال

11. uncle
العم/الخال

Tom

Lily

Alex

Emily

8. sister
الأخت

9. brother
الأخ

12. cousin
ابن/بنت العم/ـة أو الخال/ـة

7. (Min and Lu's)
grandson
الحفيد

Berta

Mario

Ana Garcia's
Family

13. mother-in-law
الحماة

14. father-in-law
الحمو

Ana

Marta

Carlos

Tito

20. (Tito's) wife
الزوجة

15. sister-in-law
السلفة

16. brother-in-law
أخو الزوج أو الزوجة

19. husband
الزوج

Alice

Eddie

Sara

Felix

17. niece
ابنة الأخ/ الأخت

18. nephew
ابن الأخ/ الأخت

21. daughter
الإبنة

22. son
الإبن

More vocabulary

Lily and Emily are Min and Lu's **granddaughters.**
Daniel is Min and Lu's **son-in-law.**
Ana is Berta and Mario's **daughter-in-law.**

Share your answers.

1. How many brothers and sisters do you have?
2. What number son or daughter are you?
3. Do you have any children?

Lisa Smith's Family

23. married
متزوج/متزوجة

Carol Dan

Lisa

24. divorced
مطلق/مطلقة

25. single mother
أم عزباء

26. single father
أب أعزب

Rick Carol

27. remarried
متزوج للمرة الثانية

Dan Sue

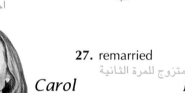

Rick Carol

28. stepfather
زوج الأم

David Mary

29. half brother
أخ غير شقيق

30. half sister
أخت غير شقيقة

Lisa

Dan Sue

31. stepmother
زوجة الأب

Kim Bill

32. stepsister
أخت من زوج الأم/
زوجة الأب

33. stepbrother
أخ من زوج الأم/
زوجة الأب

More vocabulary

Carol is Dan's **former wife**.

Sue is Dan's **wife**.

Dan is Carol's **former husband**.

Rick is Carol's **husband**.

Lisa is the **stepdaughter** of both Rick and Sue.

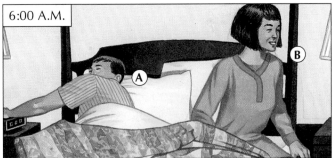

6:00 A.M.

6:30 A.M.

7:00 A.M.

7:30 A.M.

8:00 A.M.

10:00 A.M.

4:30 P.M.

5:00 P.M.

A. wake up
يستيقظ/تستيقظ

B. get up
يقوم/تقوم من السرير

C. take a shower
يستحم/تستحم

D. get dressed
يرتدي/ترتدي الثياب

E. eat breakfast
يتناول/تتناول الفطار

F. make lunch
يحضر/تحضر الغذاء

G. take the children to school
يأخذ/تأخذ الأطفال إلى المدرسة

H. take the bus to school
يركب/تركب الباص إلى المدرسة

I. drive to work/**go** to work
يذهب/تذهب إلى العمل

J. be in school
يكون/تكون في المدرسة

K. work
يعمل/تعمل

L. go to the market
يذهب/تذهب إلى السوق

M. leave work
يترك/تترك العمل

Grammar point: 3rd person singular

For **he** and **she**, we add **-s** or **-es** to the verb.

He/She wakes up.

He/She watches TV.

These verbs are different (irregular):

be   *He/She **is** in school at 10:00 a.m.*

have   *He/She **has** dinner at 6:30 p.m.*

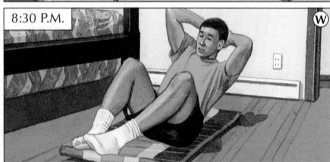

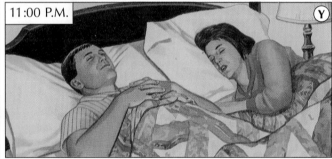

N. clean the house
تنظف المنزل

O. pick up the children
يحضر الأطفال

P. cook dinner
تحضّر العشاء

Q. come home/**get** home
يرجع/ يصل إلى المنزل

R. have dinner
يتناول/تتناول العشاء

S. watch TV
تشاهد التلفزيون

T. do homework
يعمل الواجب المدرسي

U. relax
يسترخي

V. read the paper
تقرأ الصحيفة

W. exercise
يتمرن رياضة

X. go to bed
يذهب/تذهب للفراش

Y. go to sleep
ينام/تنام

Talk about your daily routine.

I take a shower in the morning.

I go to school in the evening.

I go to bed at 11 o'clock.

Share your answers.

1. Who makes dinner in your family?

2. Who goes to the market?

3. Who goes to work?

A. **be born**
يولد

B. **start** school
يدخل المدرسة

C. **immigrate**
يهاجر

D. **graduate**
يتخرج

E. **learn** to drive
يتعلم قيادة السيارات

F. **join** the army
يلتحق بالجندية

G. **get** a job
يحصل على وظيفة

H. **become** a citizen
يصبح مواطنا

I. **rent** an apartment
يستأجر شقة

J. **go** to college
يلتحق بالجامعة

K. **fall** in love
يقع في حب فتاة

L. **get** married
يتزوج

Grammar point: past tense

start		immigrate	
learn		graduate	
join	+ed	move	+d
rent		retire	
travel		die	

These verbs are different (irregular):

be	— was	have	— had
get	— got	buy	— bought
become	— became		
go	— went		
fall	— fell		

28

 1960

 1967

M. have a baby
تنجب طفلا
N. travel
يسافر/تسافر

 1971

 1971

O. buy a house
يشتري/تشتري منزلا
P. move
ينتقل/تنتقل

 1985

 1997

Q. have a grandchild
يُرزق/ترزق بحفيد
R. die
يموت/تموت

1. birth certificate
شهادة ميلاد
2. diploma
شهادة دبلوم
3. Resident Alien card
بطاقة إقامة

4. driver's license
رخصة قيادة
5. Social Security card
بطاقة ضمان اجتماعي
6. Certificate of Naturalization
شهادة جنسية

7. college degree
شهادة جامعية
8. marriage license
رخصة زواج
9. passport
جواز سفر

More vocabulary

When a husband dies, his wife becomes a **widow**.

When a wife dies, her husband becomes a **widower**.

When older people stop working, we say they **retire**.

Talk about yourself.

I was born in 1968.

I learned to drive in 1987.

I immigrated in 1990.

1. hot
   حار
2. thirsty
   ظامئ/عطشان
3. sleepy
   نعسان/ـة

4. cold
   بردان/ـة
5. hungry
   جائع/ـة
6. full
   شبعان/ـة

7. comfortable
   مرتاح/ـة
8. uncomfortable
   غير مرتاح/ـة
9. disgusted
   مشمئزّ/ة
10. calm
    هادئ/هادئة
11. nervous
    متوتر/ـة

12. in pain
    مُصاب بألم
13. worried
    قلق/ـة
14. sick
    مريض/ـة
15. well
    معافى/معافيه
16. relieved
    منفرج/ـة

17. hurt
    مستاء/مكسور الخاطر
18. lonely
    وحيد
19. in love
    محب – عاشق

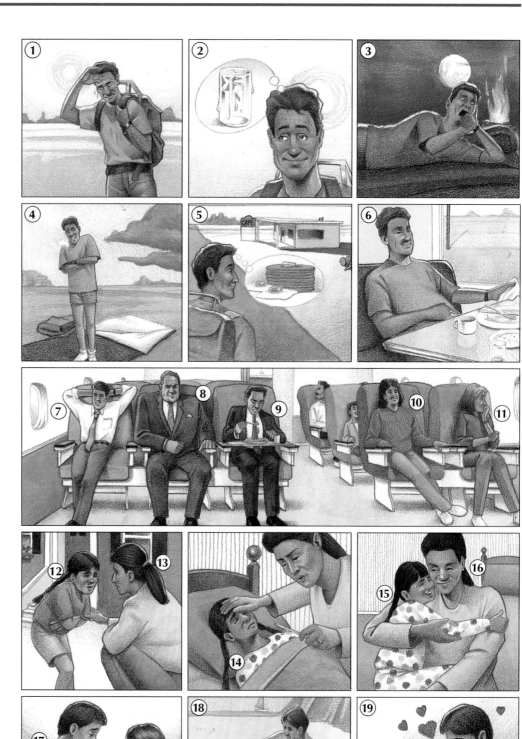

More vocabulary

furious: very angry

terrified: very scared

overjoyed: very happy

exhausted: very tired

starving: very hungry

humiliated: very embarrassed

Talk about your feelings.

I feel <u>happy</u> when I see <u>my friends</u>.

I feel <u>homesick</u> when I think about <u>my family</u>.

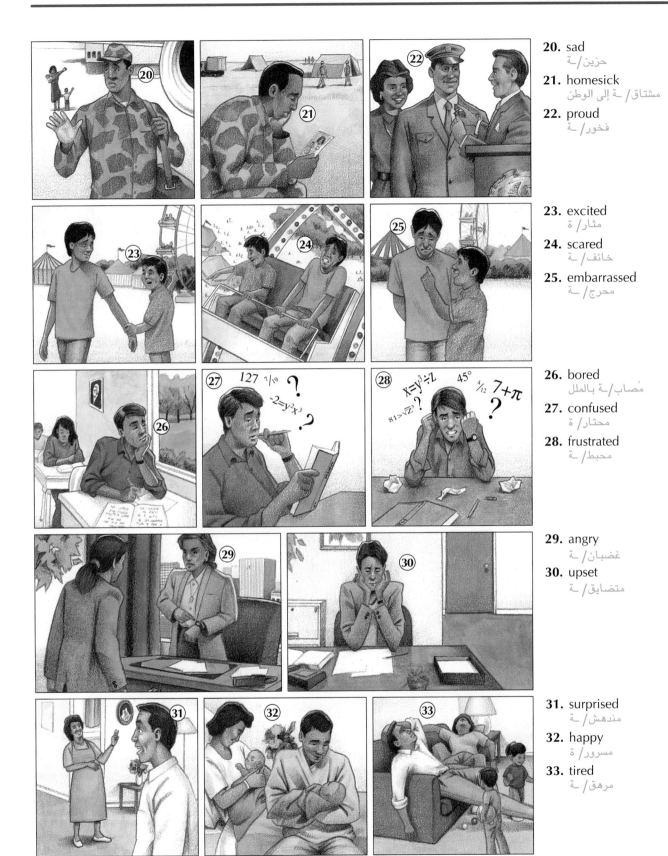

20. sad
حزين/ ـة
21. homesick
مشتاق/ ـة إلى الوطن
22. proud
فخور/ ـة

23. excited
مثار/ ة
24. scared
خائف/ ـة
25. embarrassed
محرج/ ـة

26. bored
مُصاب/ ـة بالملل
27. confused
محتار/ ة
28. frustrated
محبط/ ـة

29. angry
غضبان/ ـة
30. upset
متضايق/ ـة

31. surprised
مندهش/ ـة
32. happy
مسرور/ ة
33. tired
مرهق/ ـة

Use the new language.

Look at **Clothing I,** page **64,** and answer the questions.

1. How does the runner feel?

2. How does the man at the bus stop feel?

3. How does the woman at the bus stop feel?

4. How do the teenagers feel?

5. How does the little boy feel?

The Ceremony

1. graduating class	**5.** podium	**9.** guest speaker	**B. applaud / clap**
دفعة التخرج	المنصة	ضيف الشرف	يصفق / تصفق
2. gown	**6.** graduate	**10.** audience	**C. cry**
رداء التخرج	متخرج/ ـة	الجمهور	يبكي/ تبكي
3. cap	**7.** diploma	**11.** photographer	**D. take** a picture
قبعة التخرج	الشهادة	المصور	يلتقط/ تلتقط صورة
4. stage	**8.** valedictorian	**A. graduate**	**E. give** a speech
المسرح	ملقي خطبة الوداع	يتخرج / تتخرج	يخطب / تخطب

Talk about what the people in the pictures are doing.

She is ⎡ tak**ing** a picture.
       ⎢ giv**ing** a speech.
       ⎢ smil**ing**.
       ⎣ laugh**ing**.

He is ⎡ mak**ing** a toast.
       ⎣ clap**ping**.

They are ⎡ graduat**ing**.
          ⎢ hug**ging**.
          ⎢ kiss**ing**.
          ⎣ applaud**ing**.

32

The Party

12. caterer
متعهد تقديم الطعام

13. buffet
بوفيه/ السفرة

14. guests
ضيوف

15. banner
راية

16. dance floor
ساحة الرقص

17. DJ (disc jockey)
موزع الموسيقى

18. gifts
هدايا

F. kiss
يقبّل/ تقبل

G. hug
يعانق/ تعانق

H. laugh
يضحك/ تضحك

I. make a toast
يشرب/ تشرب نخب

J. dance
يرقص/ ترقص

Share your answers.

1. Did you ever go to a graduation? Whose?

2. Did you ever give a speech? Where?

3. Did you ever hear a great speaker? Where?

4. Did you ever go to a graduation party?

5. What do you like to eat at parties?

6. Do you like to dance at parties?

33

Places to Live أماكن للسكن

1. the city/an urban area
المدينة

2. the suburbs
الضاحية

3. a small town
بلد صغير

4. the country/a rural area
الريف

5. apartment building
بناية شقق

6. house
بيت

7. townhouse
بيت مؤلف من أكثر من طابق

8. mobile home
بيت متنقل

9. college dormitory
مساكن الطلبة

10. shelter
ملجأ

11. nursing home
بيت للعجزة

12. ranch
مزرعة

13. farm
حقل

More vocabulary

duplex house: a house divided into two homes

condominium: an apartment building where each apartment is owned separately

co-op: an apartment building owned by the residents

Share your answers.

1. Do you like where you live?
2. Where did you live in your country?
3. What types of housing are there near your school?

34

Renting an apartment استئجار شقة

A. look for a new apartment
تبحث عن شقة جديدة

B. talk to the manager
تتحدث مع المدير

C. sign a rental agreement
توقع عقد الإيجار

D. move in
تنتقل إلى الشقة

E. unpack
تفرّغ المحتويات

F. pay the rent
تدفع الإيجار

Buying a house شراء منزل

G. talk to the Realtor
يتحدث/ تتحدث مع السمسار

H. make an offer
يقدم/ تقدم عرضا

I. get a loan
يحصل/ تحصل على قرض

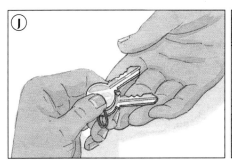

J. take ownership
يحصل/ تحصل على الملكية

K. arrange the furniture
يرتب/ ترتب الأثاث

L. pay the mortgage
يدفع/ تدفع الرهن العقاري

More vocabulary

lease: a rental agreement for a specific period of time
utilities: gas, water, and electricity for the home

Practice talking to an apartment manager.

How much is the rent?
Are utilities included?
When can I move in?

Entrance

Laundry Room

Recreation Room

Garage

1. first floor
الطابق الأول

2. second floor
الطابق الثاني

3. third floor
الطابق الثالث

4. fourth floor
الطابق الرابع

5. roof garden
حديقة السطح

6. playground
الملعب

7. fire escape
سلم النجاة

8. intercom / speaker
نظام الاتصال الداخلي

9. security system
نظام الأمان

10. doorman
البواب

11. vacancy sign
لافتة الشقق الشاغرة

12. manager / superintendent
المدير / المشرف

13. security gate
بوابة الأمان

14. storage locker
المخزن

15. parking space
مكان لوقوف السيارات

More vocabulary

rec room: a short way of saying **recreation room**

basement: the area below the street level of an apartment or a house

Talk about where you live.

I live in Apartment 3 near the entrance.

I live in Apartment 11 on the second floor near the fire escape.

Hallway

FIRE EXIT

Entryway

Office

Lobby

16. swimming pool بركة/ حمام السباحة	**23.** fire exit مخرج حريق	**30.** doorknob قبضة الباب
17. balcony شرفة	**24.** trash chute فتحة إلقاء النفايات	**31.** key مفتاح
18. courtyard حديقة	**25.** smoke detector جهاز كشف الدخان	**32.** landlord صاحب الملك
19. air conditioner مكيف هواء	**26.** stairway بيت الدرج	**33.** tenant مستأجر
20. trash bin وعاء مهملات	**27.** peephole ثقب الباب	**34.** elevator مصعد
21. alley ممر	**28.** door chain سلسلة أمان للباب	**35.** stairs درج
22. neighbor جار	**29.** dead-bolt lock قفل بمزلاج ثابت	**36.** mailboxes صناديق البريد

Grammar point: *there is, there are*

singular: *there is*   plural: *there are*

There is a fire exit in the hallway.

There are mailboxes in the lobby.

Talk about apartments.

My apartment has <u>an elevator</u>, <u>a lobby</u>, and <u>a rec room</u>.

My apartment doesn't have <u>a pool</u> or <u>a garage</u>.

My apartment needs <u>air conditioning</u>.

A House منزل

1. floor plan خريطة لمبنى	**7.** garage door باب الكراج	**13.** steps درجات	**19.** gutter مزراب
2. backyard الحديقة الخلفية	**8.** screen door باب سلك	**14.** front walk ممر المدخل الرئيسي	**20.** roof سقف المنزل
3. fence سور	**9.** porch light مصباح الشرفة	**15.** front yard الساحة الأمامية	**21.** chimney مدخنة
4. mailbox صندوق بريد	**10.** doorbell جرس الباب	**16.** deck منصة جلوس	**22.** TV antenna هوائي تلفزيون/ انتنا
5. driveway ممر الكراج	**11.** front door الباب الأمامي	**17.** window نافذة	
6. garage كراج	**12.** storm door باب حاجز	**18.** shutter مصراع النافذة	

More vocabulary

two-story house: a house with two floors

downstairs: the bottom floor

upstairs: the part of a house above the bottom floor

Share your answers.

1. What do you like about this house?
2. What's something you don't like about the house?
3. Describe the perfect house.

38

1. hedge حاجز من الشجر	**8.** sprinkler مرشة	**15.** pruning shears مقص لتقليم الأشجار	**22.** lawn mower جزازة العشب
2. hammock أرجوحة شبكية	**9.** hose خرطوم	**16.** wheelbarrow عجلة يد	**A.** **weed** the flower bed يزيل الأعشاب الضارة
3. garbage can صندوق المهملات	**10.** compost pile كومة سماد طبيعي	**17.** watering can وعاء للرش	**B.** **water** the plants يسقي الزرع
4. leaf blower جهاز نفخ أوراق الشجر	**11.** rake مدمة لجمع الخشب	**18.** flowerpot أصيص للزهور	**C.** **mow** the lawn يجزّ العشب
5. patio furniture أثاث الفناء	**12.** hedge clippers مقلمة الشجر	**19.** flower زهرة	**D.** **plant** a tree يزرع شجرة
6. patio فناء مرصوف	**13.** shovel جاروف/ رفش	**20.** bush مجموعة شجيرات	**E.** **trim** the hedge يقلم الأشجار
7. barbecue grill شوي لحم	**14.** trowel المالج (أداة لرفع النباتات الصغيرة)	**21.** lawn مرج	**F.** **rake** the leaves يجمع أوراق الشجر

Talk about your yard and gardening.

I like to plant trees.

I don't like to weed.

I like/don't like to work in the yard/garden.

Share your answers.

1. What flowers, trees, or plants do you see in the picture? (Look at **Trees, Plants, and Flowers,** pages **128–129** for help.)

2. Do you ever use a barbecue grill to cook?

1. cabinet خزانة	**8.** shelf رف	**15.** toaster oven فرن لتحميص الخبز	**22.** counter طاولة طويلة (منضدة)
2. paper towels مناديل ورق	**9.** refrigerator ثلاجة	**16.** pot قدر طبخ	**23.** drawer درج/ جارور
3. dish drainer صفاية صحون	**10.** freezer قسم التجميد	**17.** teakettle ابريق شاي	**24.** pan مقلاة
4. dishwasher غسالة صحون/ جلاية	**11.** coffeemaker ركوة قهوة كهربائية	**18.** stove موقد	**25.** electric mixer خلاط كهربائي
5. garbage disposal وعاء للنفايات	**12.** blender خلاط	**19.** burner مضرم	**26.** food processor جهاز تحضير الماكولات
6. sink مغسلة	**13.** microwave oven مايكروويف	**20.** oven فرن	**27.** cutting board لوح تقطيع
7. toaster محمصة الخبز	**14.** electric can opener فتاحة علب كهربائية	**21.** broiler مشواة	

Talk about the location of kitchen items.

The toaster oven is *on the counter* *near the stove*.

The microwave is *above the stove*.

Share your answers.

1. Do you have a garbage disposal? a dishwasher? a microwave?

2. Do you eat in the kitchen?

㉑	㉒	㉓	㉔	㉕	㉖	㉗	㉘

1. china cabinet
خزانة الأطبـاق

2. set of dishes
طقم أطباق

3. platter
طبق كبير

4. ceiling fan
مروحة سقف

5. light fixture
ضوء مثبت

6. serving dish
طبق تقديم

7. candle
شمعة

8. candlestick
شمعدان

9. vase
زهرية

10. tray
صينية

11. teapot
ابريق شاي

12. sugar bowl
علبة سكر

13. creamer
حليب / لبن

14. saltshaker
مذرة الملح/ مملحة

15. pepper shaker
مذرة الفلفل

16. dining room chair
كرسي حجرة الطعام

17. dining room table
طاولة حجرة الطعام

18. tablecloth
مفرش الطاولة

19. napkin
منديل المائدة

20. place mat
قطعة قماش توضع تحت الطبق

21. fork
شوكة

22. knife
سكين

23. spoon
ملعقة

24. plate
طبق

25. bowl
وعاء مجوف

26. glass
كأس

27. coffee cup
فنجان قهوة

28. mug
فنجان كبير

Practice asking for things in the dining room.

Please pass the platter.

May I have the creamer?

Could I have a fork, please?

Share your answers.

1. What are the women in the picture saying?

2. In your home, where do you eat?

3. Do you like to make dinner for your friends?

41

A Living Room   غرفـة الجلـوس

1. bookcase خزانة كتب	**8.** mantel رف المستوقد/ المدفئة	**15.** floor lamp مصباح أرضي	**22.** magazine holder حامل الجرائد
2. basket سلة	**9.** fireplace المستوقد/ المدفئة	**16.** drapes ستائر	**23.** coffee table طاولة قهوة
3. track lighting ضوء موجه	**10.** fire نار	**17.** window نافذة	**24.** armchair/easy chair كرسي ذو ذراعين
4. lightbulb لمبة	**11.** fire screen حاجب النار	**18.** plant نبتة	**25.** love seat أريكة مزدوجة
5. ceiling سقف	**12.** logs قطع خشب للحرق	**19.** sofa/couch أريكة	**26.** TV (television) تليفزيون
6. wall حائط	**13.** wall unit أثاث مثبت على الحائط	**20.** throw pillow وسادة للزينة	**27.** carpet سجادة
7. painting دهان	**14.** stereo system جهاز ستيريو	**21.** end table طاولة جانبية	

Use the new language.

Look at **Colors**, page **12**, and describe this room.

There is a gray sofa and a gray armchair.

Talk about your living room.

In my living room I have a sofa, two chairs, and a coffee table.

I don't have a fireplace or a wall unit.

1. hamper سبت/ سلة الملابس	**8.** towel rack حمالة فوط/ مناشف	**15.** toilet paper ورق المرحاض/ تواليت	**22.** sink حوض/ مغسلة
2. bathtub بانيو	**9.** tile قرميد	**16.** toilet brush فرشاة المرحاض	**23.** soap صابون
3. rubber mat حصيرة مطاطية	**10.** showerhead رأس الدش	**17.** toilet مرحاض	**24.** soap dish حاملة الصابون
4. drain مصرف المياه	**11.** (mini)blinds ستائر	**18.** mirror مرآة	**25.** wastebasket سلة المهملات
5. hot water ماء ساخن	**12.** bath towel منشفة للإستحمام	**19.** medicine cabinet مستودع للأدوية	**26.** scale ميزان
6. faucet حنفية	**13.** hand towel فوطة لليد	**20.** toothbrush فرشاة أسنان	**27.** bath mat حصيرة الحمــام
7. cold water ماء بارد	**14.** washcloth فوطة/ منشفة صغيرة	**21.** toothbrush holder حامل فرشاة الأسنان	

More vocabulary

half bath: a bathroom without a shower or bathtub

linen closet: a closet or cabinet for towels and sheets

stall shower: a shower without a bathtub

Share your answers.

1. Do you turn off the water when you brush your teeth? wash your hair? shave?

2. Does your bathroom have a bathtub or a stall shower?

1. mirror مرآة	**8.** bed سرير	**15.** headboard رأس السرير	**22.** dust ruffle كشكش مانع للغبار
2. dresser/bureau خزانة ملابس بمرآة	**9.** pillow وسادة	**16.** clock radio مذياع ذو ساعة	**23.** rug سجادة
3. drawer درج/ جارور	**10.** pillowcase كيس وسادة	**17.** lamp مصباح	**24.** floor أرض الحجرة
4. closet دولاب/ خزانة	**11.** bedspread مفرش سرير/ شرشف	**18.** lampshade قبعة المصباح	**25.** mattress فراش
5. curtains ستائر	**12.** blanket بطانية	**19.** light switch مفتاح الضوء	**26.** box spring صندوق زنبركي تحت الفراش
6. window shade حاجب للضوء	**13.** flat sheet ملاءة	**20.** outlet مأخذ التيار	**27.** bed frame قاعدة الفراش
7. photograph صورة	**14.** fitted sheet ملاءة مفصّلة	**21.** night table طاولة جانبية	

Use the new language.

Describe this room. (See **Describing Things**, page **11**, for help.)

I see a soft pillow and a beautiful bedspread.

Share your answers.

1. What is your favorite thing in your bedroom?

2. Do you have a clock in your bedroom? Where is it?

3. Do you have a mirror in your bedroom? Where is it?

1. bunk bed سرير مزدوج	7. bumper pad حاجز وقائي للطفل	13. diaper pail دلو أحفضة	19. cradle سرير هزاز
2. comforter لحاف	8. chest of drawers خزانة ذات ادراج	14. dollhouse بيت للدمي	20. coloring book كتاب تلوين
3. night-light ضوء سهاري	9. baby monitor جهاز مراقبة الطفل	15. blocks مكعبات	21. crayons أقلام شمع/ تلاوين
4. mobile لعبة بزنبرك دوارة	10. teddy bear دب تيدي	16. ball كرة	22. puzzle لغز
5. wallpaper ورق حائط	11. smoke detector جهاز كشف الدخان	17. picture book كتاب مصوِر	23. stuffed animals حيوانات لعبة
6. crib سرير طفل رضيع	12. changing table طاولة لتغيير ملابس الرضيع	18. doll دمية	24. toy chest صندوق اللعب

Talk about where items are in the room.

The dollhouse is near *the coloring book*.

The teddy bear is on *the chest of drawers*.

Share your answers.

1. Do you think this is a good room for children? Why?

2. What toys did you play with when you were a child?

3. What children's stories do you know?

A. **dust** the furniture
تمسح الغبار عن الأثاث

B. **recycle** the newspapers
تعد الصحف للاستعمال ثانية

C. **clean** the oven
تنظف الفرن

D. **wash** the windows
تغسل النوافذ

E. **sweep** the floor
يكنس الأرض

F. **empty** the wastebasket
يفرغ سلة المهملات

G. **make** the bed
يرتب الفراش

H. **put away** the toys
يضع اللعب في مكانها

I. **vacuum** the carpet
ينظف السجادة بالمكسنة الكهربائية

J. **mop** the floor
يمسح الأرضية

K. **polish** the furniture
تلمِّع الأثاث

L. **scrub** the floor
تنظف الأرض بالفرشاة

M. **wash** the dishes
يغسل الصحون

N. **dry** the dishes
تجفف الصحون

O. **wipe** the counter
تمسح الطاولة

P. **change** the sheets
تغير الملاءات

Q. **take out** the garbage
يلقي النفايات

Talk about yourself.

I wash the dishes every day.
I change the sheets every week.
I never dry the dishes.

Share your answers.

1. Who does the housework in your family?
2. What is your favorite cleaning job?
3. What is your least favorite cleaning job?

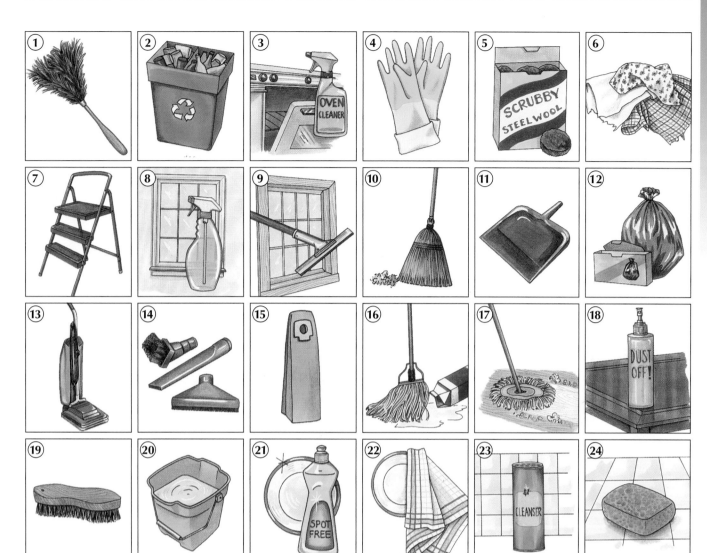

Cleaning Supplies

1. feather duster ريشة التنظيف	**9.** squeegee مساحة مطاطية
2. recycling bin نفايات قابلة للتصنيع	**10.** broom مقشة/ مكنسة
3. oven cleaner منظف الفرن	**11.** dustpan جاروف/ لقاطة الكناسة
4. rubber gloves قفاز مطاطي	**12.** trash bags أكياس المهملات
5. steel-wool soap pads قطع سلك للتنظيف	**13.** vacuum cleaner مكنسة كهربائية
6. rags أقمشة للتنظيف	**14.** vacuum cleaner attachments قطع اضافية للمكنسة الكهربائية
7. stepladder سلم صغير/ السيبة	**15.** vacuum cleaner bag كيس للمكنسة الكهربائية
8. glass cleaner منظف الزجاج	**16.** wet mop ممسحة مبتلة

17. dust mop
ممسحة غبار

18. furniture polish
ملمع الأثاث

19. scrub brush
فرشاة قاسية

20. bucket/pail
دلو/ سطل

21. dishwashing liquid
مسحوق لتنظيف الصحون

22. dish towel
فوطة لتجفيف الصحون

23. cleanser
منظف ومطهر

24. sponge
اسفنجة

Practice asking for the items.

I want to <u>wash the windows</u>.
Please hand me <u>the squeegee</u>.

I have to <u>sweep the floor</u>.
Can you get me <u>the broom</u>, please?

1. The water heater is **not working**.
   سخان المياه لا يعمل.
2. The power is **out**.
   التيار الكهربائي مقطوع.
3. The roof is **leaking**.
   السطح يرشح.
4. The wall is **cracked**.
   الحائط مشقوق.
5. The window is **broken**.
   النافذة مكسورة.

6. The lock is **broken**.
   القفل مكسور.
7. The steps are **broken**.
   الدرج مكسور.
8. roofer
   مصلح السطح
9. electrician
   كهربائي
10. repair person
    مرمم

11. locksmith
    مصلح أقفال
12. carpenter
    نجار
13. fuse box
    صندوق الصمامة الكهربائية
14. gas meter
    عداد الغاز

Use the new language.
Look at **Tools and Building Supplies,** pages **150–151.**
Name the tools you use for household repairs.

I use a hammer and nails to fix a broken step.
I use a wrench to repair a dripping faucet.

15. The furnace is **broken**.
الفرن متعطل.

16. The faucet is **dripping**.
الحنفية تقطر.

17. The sink is **overflowing**.
المغسلة فائضة.

18. The toilet is **stopped up**.
المرحاض مسدود.

19. The pipes are **frozen**.
المواسير متجمدة.

20. plumber
سمكري / سباك

21. exterminator
شخص متخصص في إبادة الحشرات

Household pests
حشرات منزلية

22. termite(s)
نمله بيضاء (نمل أبيض)

23. flea(s)
برغوث (براغيث)

24. ant(s)
نملة (نمل)

25. cockroach(es)
صرصور (صراصير)

26. mice*
فأر (فئران)

27. rat(s)
جرذ (جرذان)

*Note: *one mouse, two mice*

More vocabulary

fix: to repair something that is broken

exterminate: to kill household pests

pesticide: a chemical that is used to kill household pests

Share your answers.

1. Who does household repairs in your home?

2. What is the worst problem a home can have?

3. What is the most expensive problem a home can have?

1. grapes
عنب

2. pineapples
اناناس

3. bananas
موز

4. apples
تفاح

5. peaches
دراق/ خوخ

6. pears
كمثرى

7. apricots
مشمش

8. plums
خوخ/ برقوق

9. grapefruit
ليمون الجنة/ كريفوت

10. oranges
برتقال

11. lemons
ليمون

12. limes
الليم

13. tangerines
اليوسفي

14. avocadoes
الافوكاته

15. cantaloupes
الشمـام

16. cherries
كرز

17. strawberries
فراولة/ فريز

18. raspberries
توتة العليق

19. blueberries
ثمر العنبة

20. papayas
ثمر الببايا

21. mangoes
مانجه

22. coconuts
جوز الهند

23. nuts
مكسرات

24. watermelons
بطيخ

25. dates
بلح/ تمر

26. prunes
برقوق مجفف

27. raisins
زبيب

28. not ripe
غير ناضج

29. ripe
ناضج

30. rotten
عفن

Language note: *a bunch of*

We say *a bunch of grapes* and *a bunch of bananas*.

Share your answers.

1. Which fruits do you put in a fruit salad?

2. Which fruits are sold in your area in the summer?

3. What fruits did you have in your country?

1. lettuce
خس

2. cabbage
كرنب/ ملفوف

3. carrots
جزر

4. zucchini
القرع الصيفي

5. radishes
فجل

6. beets
شمندر

7. sweet peppers
فلفل حلو

8. chili peppers
فلفل حار

9. celery
كرفس

10. parsley
البقدونس

11. spinach
سبانخ

12. cucumbers
خيار

13. squash
القرع

14. turnips
لفت

15. broccoli
نوع من القرنبيط (بروكلي)

16. cauliflower
قرنبيط

17. scallions
الكراث/ بصل أخضر

18. eggplants
باذنجان

19. peas
بازلا

20. artichokes
خرشوف

21. potatoes
بطاطا

22. yams
اليام – بطاطا حلوة

23. tomatoes
طماطم/ بندورة

24. asparagus
هليون

25. string beans
فاصوليا

26. mushrooms
فطر

27. corn
ذرة

28. onions
بصل

29. garlic
ثوم

Language note: *a bunch of, a head of*

We say *a bunch of carrots, a bunch of celery,* and *a bunch of spinach.*

We say *a head of lettuce, a head of cabbage,* and *a head of cauliflower.*

Share your answers.

1. Which vegetables do you eat raw? cooked?

2. Which vegetables need to be in the refrigerator?

3. Which vegetables don't need to be in the refrigerator?

Beef   لحم بقر

1. roast beef
قطعة لحم للشوي

2. steak
شريحة لحم

3. stewing beef
لحم للسلق

4. ground beef
لحم مفروم

5. beef ribs
ضلوع لحم

6. veal cutlets
شريحة لحم عجل

7. liver
كبدة

8. tripe
الكرش

Pork   لحم الخنزير

9. ham
فخذ خنزير

10. pork chops
شرائح لحم خنزير

11. bacon
لحم خنزير مملح

12. sausage
نقانق

Lamb   لحم خروف

13. lamb shanks
ساق الخروف

14. leg of lamb
فخذة خروف

15. lamb chops
شرائح خروف

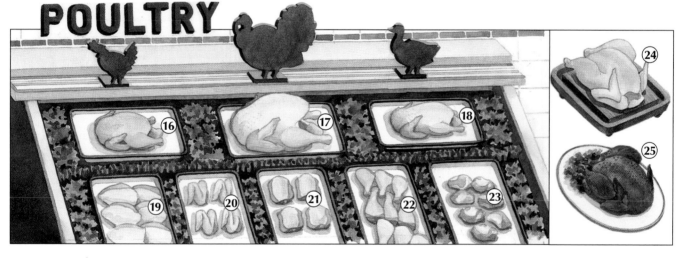

16. chicken
دجاجة

17. turkey
ديك رومي

18. duck
بطة

19. breasts
صدور

20. wings
أجنحـة

21. thighs
فخذات

22. drumsticks
وصلة الفخذ بالكاحل

23. gizzards
القوانص

24. raw chicken
دجاج نيء

25. cooked chicken
دجاجة مطهية

More vocabulary

vegetarian: a person who doesn't eat meat

Meat and poultry without bones are called **boneless**.

Poultry without skin is called **skinless**.

Share your answers.

1. What kind of meat do you eat most often?

2. What kind of meat do you use in soup?

3. What part of the chicken do you like the most?

DELI

1. white bread
خبز أبيض

2. wheat bread
خبز من دقيق القمح

3. rye bread
خبز الجاودار

4. smoked turkey
ديك رومي مدخن

5. salami
سجق السلامي

6. pastrami
بسطرمة

7. roast beef
قطعة لحم للشوي

8. corned beef
لحم مملح

9. American cheese
جبن أمريكي

10. cheddar cheese
جبن شدر

11. Swiss cheese
جبن سويسري

12. jack cheese
جبن جاك

13. potato salad
سلطة بطاطس

14. coleslaw
سلطة كرنب

15. pasta salad
سلطة معكرونة

SEAFOOD

Fish   الأسماك

16. trout
سمك التروتة المرقط

17. catfish
سمك الصلور

18. whole salmon
سمك السلمون

19. salmon steak
شريحة سلمون

20. halibut
سمك الهلبوت المفلطح

21. filet of sole
شرائح سمك موسى

Shellfish   المحــار

22. crab
سرطان البحر

23. lobster
جراد البحر

24. shrimp
قريدس/ جمبري

25. scallops
اسقلوب/ المحار

26. mussels
بلح البحر

27. oysters
محار رخوي

28. clams
صدف البطلينوس

29. **fresh** fish
سمك طازج

30. **frozen** fish
سمك مجمد

Practice ordering a sandwich.

I'd like <u>roast beef</u> and <u>American cheese</u> on <u>rye bread</u>.

Tell what you want on it.

Please put <u>tomato</u>, <u>lettuce</u>, <u>onions</u>, and <u>mustard</u> on it.

Share your answers.

1. Do you like to eat fish?

2. Do you buy fresh or frozen fish?

53

1. bottle return
اعادة الزجاجات الفارغة

2. meat and poultry section
قسم اللحوم والدواجن

3. shopping cart
عربة التسوق

4. canned goods
المعلبات

5. aisle
ممر

6. baked goods
المخبوزات

7. shopping basket
سلة التسوق

8. manager
المدير

9. dairy section
قسم الألبان

10. pet food
طعام الحيوانات

11. produce section
قسم الخضروات

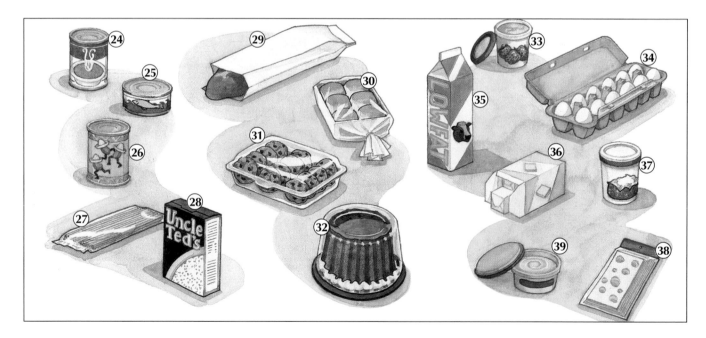

24. soup
شوربة

25. tuna
علبة سمك التونة

26. beans
فول

27. spaghetti
معكرونة

28. rice
أرز

29. bread
خبز

30. rolls
أقراص خبز

31. cookies
كعك رقيق محلى

32. cake
كعكة

33. yogurt
زبادي/ لبن

34. eggs
بيض

35. milk
لبن/ حليب

36. butter
زبدة

37. sour cream
كريما حامضة

38. cheese
جبن

39. margarine
المرغرين – سمن نباتي

12. frozen foods
أطعمة مجمدة

13. baking products
منتجات للخبز

14. paper products
منتجات ورقية

15. beverages
المشروبات – المرطبات

16. snack foods
الوجبات الخفيفة

17. checkstand
مركز الدفع

18. cash register
ماكينة تسجيل الدفع

19. checker
امين/ ـة الصندوق

20. line
صف

21. bagger
معبًا أكياس

22. paper bag
كيس ورق

23. plastic bag
كيس بلاستيك

40. potato chips
رقائق بطاطس مقلية

41. candy bar
حلوى

42. gum
لبان/ علكة

43. frozen vegetables
خضروات مجمدة

44. ice cream
جيلاتي/ بوظة

45. flour
دقيق

46. spices
بهارات

47. cake mix
خليط كعكة جاف

48. sugar
سكر

49. oil
زيت

50. apple juice
عصير تفاح

51. instant coffee
قهوة سريعة الذوقان

52. soda
صودا

53. bottled water
مياه معدنية

54. plastic wrap
رقاقة بلاستيك للتغليف

55. aluminum foil
صفائح الومنيوم للتغليف

   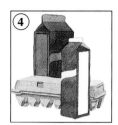

1. bottle
زجاجة

2. jar
مرطبان

3. can
علبة معدنية

4. carton
علبة كرتون

5. container
حاوية/ وعاء

6. box
علبة

7. bag
كيس

8. package
رزمة

9. six-pack
ستة علب

10. loaf
رغيف

11. roll
لفة

12. tube
أنبوب

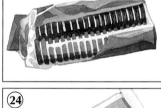 

13. a bottle of soda
زجاجة صودا

14. a jar of jam
مرطبان مربى

15. a can of soup
علبة شوربة

16. a carton of eggs
علبة كرتون من البيض

17. a container of cottage cheese
إناء جبن حلوم

18. a box of cereal
علبة حبوب (سيريال)

19. a bag of flour
كيس دقيق

20. a package of cookies
رزمة بسكوت

21. a six-pack of soda
ستة علب من الصودا

22. a loaf of bread
رغيف خبز

23. a roll of paper towels
لفة من ورق التواليت

24. a tube of toothpaste
أنبوبة معجون أسنان

Grammar point: *How much? How many?*

Some foods can be counted: *one apple, two apples.*

How many apples do you need? I need ***two*** apples.

Some foods cannot be counted, like liquids, grains, spices, or dairy foods. For these, count containers: *one box of rice, two boxes of rice.*

How much rice do you need? I need ***two boxes.***

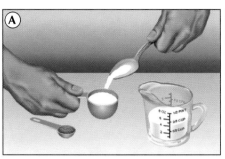

A. Measure the ingredients.
تعاير المقادير.

B. Weigh the food.
تزن الطعام.

1 cup = 237 milliliters

C. Convert the measurements.
تحوّل المعايير.

Liquid measures مقاييس السوائل

① 1 fl. oz. أونس ١

② 1 c. كوب ١

③ 1 pt. باينت ١

④ 1 qt. كوارت ١

1 gal. جالون ١ ⑤

Dry measures مقاييس المواد الجافة

⑥ 1 tsp. ملعقة شاي ١

⑦ 1 TBS. ملعقة طعام ١

⑧ 1/4 c. كوب (ربع) ١/٤

⑨ 1/2 c. كوب (نصف) ١/٢

⑩ 1 c. كوب ١

Weight الوزن

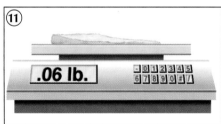
⑪ .06 lb.

⑫ 1.00 lb.

1. a fluid ounce of water
أونس ماء

2. a cup of oil
كوب زيت

3. a pint of yogurt
باينت زبادي/ لبن

4. a quart of milk
كوارت لبن/ حليب

5. a gallon of apple juice
جالون عصير تفاح

6. a teaspoon of salt
ملعقة شاي من ملح

7. a tablespoon of sugar
ملعقة طعام من السكر

8. a 1/4 cup of brown sugar
١/٤ (ربع) كوب سكر بني

9. a 1/2 cup of raisins
١/٢ (نصف) كوب زبيب

10. a cup of flour
كوب من الدقيق

11. an ounce of cheese
أونس من الجبن

12. a pound of roast beef
باوند من شرائح لحم البقر

VOLUME
1 fl. oz. = 30 milliliters (ml.)
1 c. = 237 ml.
1 pt. = .47 liters (l.)
1 qt. = .95 l.
1 gal. = 3.79 l.

EQUIVALENCIES
3 tsp. = 1 TBS.	2 c. = 1 pt.
2 TBS. = 1 fl. oz.	2 pt. = 1 qt.
8 fl. oz. = 1 c.	4 qt. = 1 gal.

WEIGHT
1 oz. = 28.35 grams (g.)
1 lb. = 453.6 g.
2.205 lbs. = 1 kilogram
1 lb. = 16 oz.

Scrambled eggs بيض مقلي

A. Break 3 eggs.
يكسر/ تكسر ٣ بيضات.

B. Beat well.
يخفق/ تخفق جيدا.

C. Grease the pan.
يزيت/ تزيت المقلاة.

D. Pour the eggs into the pan.
يصب/ تصب البيض في المقلاة.

E. Stir.
يحرّك/ تحرّك الطعام.

F. Cook until done.
يطهو/ تطهو الطعام حتى ينضج.

Vegetable casserole تحضير طبق الخضار

G. Chop the onions.
يقطّع/ تقطّع البصل.

H. Sauté the onions.
يقلي/ تقلي البصل بسرعه.

I. Steam the broccoli.
يطبخ/ تطبخ البروكلي على البخار.

J. Grate the cheese.
يبشر/ تبشر الجبن.

K. Mix the ingredients.
يخلط/ تخلط المقادير.

L. Bake at 350° for 45 minutes.
يضع/ تضع الطبق في فرن حرارته ٣٥٠ لـ ٤٥ دقيقة.

Chicken soup شورية الدجاج

M. Cut up the chicken.
يقطع/ تقطع الدجاجة.

N. Peel the carrots.
يقشّر/ تقشّر الجزر.

O. Slice the carrots.
يقطع/ تقطع الجزر.

P. Boil the chicken.
يسلق/ تسلق الدجاجة.

Q. Add the vegetables.
يضيف/ تضيف الخضار.

R. Simmer for 1 hour.
يطهو/ تطهو ببطء لمدة ساعة.

 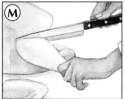 

Five ways to cook chicken خمس طرق لتحضير الدجاج

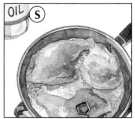   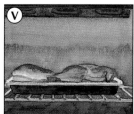 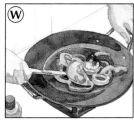

S. fry
يقلي/ تقلي

T. barbecue/grill
يشوي/ تشوي

U. roast
يضع/ تضع في الفرن

V. broil
يضع/تضع على المشواة

W. stir-fry
يقلي/ تقلي مع التحريك

Talk about the way you prepare these foods.

I *fry* eggs.

I *bake* potatoes.

Share your answers.

1. What are popular ways in your country to make rice? vegetables? meat?

2. What is your favorite way to cook chicken?

1. can opener
   فتاحة علب

2. grater
   مبشرة

3. plastic storage
   container
   علبة تخزين بلاستيك

4. steamer
   وعاء الطهي بالبخار

5. frying pan
   مقلاة

6. pot
   إناء

7. ladle
   مغرفة

8. double boiler
   إناء للغلي مزدوج

9. wooden spoon
   ملعقة من خشب

10. garlic press
    معصرة ثوم

11. casserole dish
    طبق كبير

12. carving knife
    سكين لتقطيع اللحم

13. roasting pan
    إناء شوي

14. roasting rack
    شبكة للشوي

15. vegetable peeler
    قشارة خضروات

16. paring knife
    سكين تقشير

17. colander
    مصفاة

18. kitchen timer
    ساعة مطبخ

19. spatula
    مغرفة / ملعقة مبسطة

20. eggbeater
    مخفقة بيض

21. whisk
    مخفقة

22. strainer
    مصفاة

23. tongs
    ملقطة

24. lid
    غطاء

25. saucepan
    قدر صغير

26. cake pan
    إناء الكعك

27. cookie sheet
    صينية لخبز الحلوى

28. pie pan
    صينية فطائر

29. pot holders
    ممسك اناء ساخن

30. rolling pin
    مرقاق العجين / شوبك

31. mixing bowl
    وعاء خلط

Talk about how to use the utensils.

You use a peeler to peel potatoes.

You use a pot to cook soup.

Use the new language.

Look at **Food Preparation**, page 58.

Name the different utensils you see.

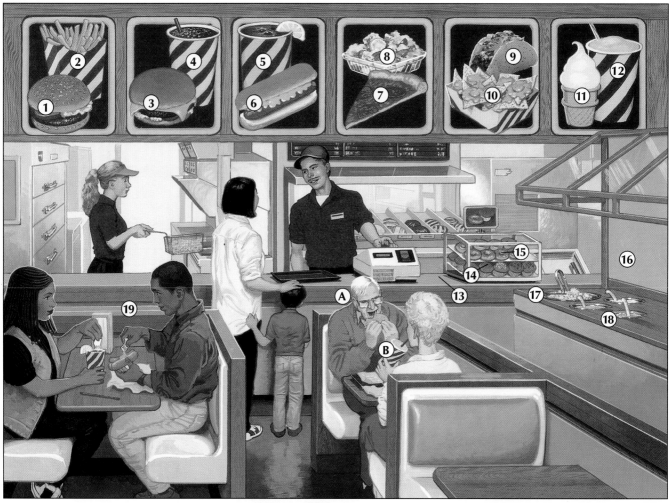

1. hamburger
هامبورجر

2. french fries
بطاطس مقلية

3. cheeseburger
هامبورجر مع الجبن

4. soda
صودا

5. iced tea
شاي مثلج

6. hot dog
هوت دوج

7. pizza
بيتزا

8. green salad
سلطة خس

9. taco
تاكو

10. nachos
ناتشوز

11. frozen yogurt
زبادي مثلج/بوظة

12. milk shake
لبن/ حليب مخفوق

13. counter
طاولة طويلة

14. muffin
فطيرة مدورة

15. doughnut
دونت/ كعكة مقلية

16. salad bar
بار السلطات

17. lettuce
خس

18. salad dressing
صلصة للسلطة

19. booth
كشك

20. straw
شفاطة/ الشاروقة

21. sugar
سكر

22. sugar substitute
بديل للسكر

23. ketchup
كاتشب/ صلصة طماطم

24. mustard
الخردل

25. mayonnaise
مايونيز

26. relish
فاتح للشهية

A. eat
يأكل

B. drink
يشرب

More vocabulary

donut: doughnut (spelling variation)

condiments: relish, mustard, ketchup, mayonnaise, etc.

Share your answers.

1. What would you order at this restaurant?

2. Which fast foods are popular in your country?

3. How often do you eat fast food? Why?

Breakfast

Lunch

Dinner

Desserts

Beverages

1. **scrambled eggs**
بيض مقلي ممزوج

2. **sausage**
نقانق

3. **toast**
خبز محمص

4. **waffles**
الوافل

5. **syrup**
شراب

6. **pancakes**
فطيرة محلاة

7. **bacon**
لحم خنزير مملح

8. **grilled cheese sandwich**
سندوتش جبن مشوي

9. **chef's salad**
سلطة المطعم

10. **soup of the day**
شوربة اليوم

11. **mashed potatoes**
بطاطس مهروسة

12. **roast chicken**
دجاج مطهي في الفرن

13. **steak**
ستيك/ شريحة

14. **baked potato**
بطاطس مطهية في الفرن

15. **pasta**
معكرونة

16. **garlic bread**
خبز بالثوم

17. **fried fish**
سمك مقلي

18. **rice pilaf**
بيلاف بالأرز

19. **cake**
كعكة

20. **pudding**
حلوى البودنغ

21. **pie**
فطيرة

22. **coffee**
قهوة

23. **decaf coffee**
قهوة بدون كافيين

24. **tea**
شاي

Practice ordering from the menu.

I'd like <u>a grilled cheese sandwich</u> and <u>some soup</u>.
I'll have <u>the chef's salad</u> and <u>a cup of decaf coffee</u>.

Use the new language.
Look at **Fruit,** page **50.**

Order a slice of pie using the different fruit flavors.
Please give me a slice of <u>apple</u> pie.

A Restaurant مطعــم

1. hostess
مضيفة

2. dining room
حجرة الطعام

3. menu
قائمة الطعام

4. server / waiter
نادل/ جرسون

5. patron / diner
زبون

A. set the table
يحضّر الطاولة

B. seat the customer
تجلس الزبون

C. pour the water
يسكب الماء

D. order from the menu
يطلب من قائمة الطعام

E. take the order
يسجل الطلب

F. serve the meal
يقدم الوجبة

G. clear the table
ينظف الطاولة

H. carry the tray
يحمل الصينية

I. pay the check
يدفع/ تدفع الفاتورة

J. leave a tip
يترك/ تترك بقشيش

More vocabulary

eat out: to go to a restaurant to eat

take out: to buy food at a restaurant and take it home to eat

Practice giving commands.

Please <u>set the table</u>.

I'd like you to <u>clear the table</u>.

It's time to <u>serve the meal</u>.

6. server / waitress
نادلة / جرسونة

7. dessert tray
صينية الحلوى

8. bread basket
سلة الخبز

9. busperson
مساعد النادل / الجرسون

10. kitchen
المطبخ

11. chef
رئيس الطهاة

12. dishroom
غرفة غسل الصحون

13. dishwasher
غسالة صحون كهربائية

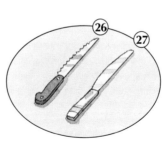

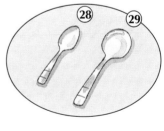

14. place setting
يرتب سفرة الطعام

15. dinner plate
صحن طعام

16. bread-and-butter plate
صحن الخبز والزبدة

17. salad plate
صحن السلطة

18. soup bowl
طبق الشوربة

19. water glass
كوب ماء

20. wine glass
كأس نبيذ

21. cup
فنجان

22. saucer
صحن الفنجان

23. napkin
منديل قماش

24. salad fork
شوكة السلطة

25. dinner fork
شوكة طعام

26. steak knife
سكين لقطع اللحم

27. knife
سكين

28. teaspoon
ملعقة شاي

29. soupspoon
ملعقة الشوربة

Talk about how you set the table in your home.

The glass is on the right.

The fork goes on the left.

The napkin is next to the plate.

Share your answers.

1. Do you know anyone who works in a restaurant? What does he or she do?

2. In your opinion, which restaurant jobs are hard? Why?

1. three-piece suit
بدلة ذو ثلاث قطع

2. suit
بدلة

3. dress
فستان

4. shirt
قميص

5. jeans
بنطلون جينز

6. sports coat
معطف سبور

7. turtleneck
بلوزة ذات ياقة عالية

8. slacks / pants
بنطلون

9. blouse
بلوزة

10. skirt
تنورة

11. pullover sweater
بلوفر

12. T-shirt
قميص تي شيرت

13. shorts
بنطلون قصير/ شورت

14. sweatshirt
سترة رياضية

15. sweatpants
بنطلون رياضة

More vocabulary:

outfit: clothes that look nice together

When clothes are popular, they are **in fashion**.

Talk about what you're wearing today and what you wore yesterday.

I'm wearing a gray sweater, a red T-shirt, and blue jeans.

Yesterday I wore a green pullover sweater, a white shirt, and black slacks.

16. jumpsuit
سترة يرتديها العمال

17. uniform
زي موحد

18. jumper
مريلة

19. maternity dress
فستان حمل

20. knit shirt
قميص

21. overalls
الوزرة

22. tunic
سترة قصيرة

23. leggings
الطماق/ كساء للساق

24. vest
صدرة

25. split skirt
تنورة مضلعة

26. sports shirt
سترة رياضية

27. cardigan sweater
سترة من صوف محبوك

28. tuxedo
بدلة رسمية للرجل

29. evening gown
فستان سهرة

Use the new language.

Look at **A Graduation,** pages **32–33.**

Name the clothes you see.

The man at the podium is wearing a suit.

Share your answers.

1. Which clothes in this picture are in fashion now?

2. Who is the best-dressed person in this line? Why?

3. What do you wear when you go to the movies?

1. hat قبعة	**5.** gloves قفاز	**8.** parka سترة فرائية	**12.** earmuffs وقاء للأذن من البرد
2. overcoat معطف	**6.** cap قلنسوة	**9.** mittens قفاز من الصوف	**13.** down vest سترة طويلة
3. leather jacket سترة جلد	**7.** jacket جاكيت	**10.** ski cap قبعة التزحلق على الجليد	**14.** ski mask قناع التزحلق على الجليد
4. wool scarf / muffler وشاح		**11.** tights بنطلون ضيق جدا	**15.** down jacket جاكيت طويل

16. umbrella شمسية	**20.** trench coat معطف واقي من المطر	**24.** windbreaker سترة حاجزة للريح
17. raincoat معطف مطر	**21.** sunglasses نظارة شمس	**25.** cover-up غطاء خارجي
18. poncho معطف شبه عباءة	**22.** swimming trunks شورت للسباحة	**26.** swimsuit / bathing suit بدلة سباحة / مايوه
19. rain boots جزمة	**23.** straw hat قبعة من القش	**27.** baseball cap قبعة البيسبول

Use the new language.

Look at **Weather,** page **10.**

Name the clothing for each weather condition.

Wear a jacket when it's windy.

Share your answers.

1. Which is better in the rain, an umbrella or a poncho?

2. Which is better in the cold, a parka or a down jacket?

3. Do you have more summer clothes or winter clothes?

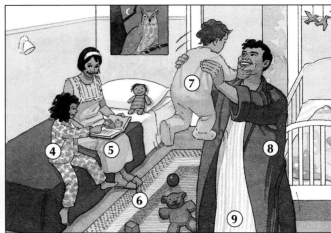

1. leotard
ثوب للرقص

2. tank top
قميص داخلي

3. bike shorts
شورت لركوب الدراجة

4. pajamas
بيجامة

5. nightgown
قميص نوم

6. slippers
شبشب/ خف

7. blanket sleeper
مريلة نوم للأطفال/ بيجامة

8. bathrobe
ثوب حمام/ برنس

9. nightshirt
قميص طويل للنوم

10. undershirt
قميص داخلي

11. long underwear
ملابس داخلية طويلة

12. boxer shorts
شورت داخلي

13. briefs
سروال

14. athletic supporter/jockstrap
سروال رياضي

15. socks
جورب قصير

16. (bikini) panties
سروال تحتي قصير نسائي

17. briefs/underpants
سروال تحتي قصير رجالي

18. girdle
مشد

19. garter belt
رباط للجورب

20. bra
صديرية للثديين

21. camisole
قميصول

22. full slip
سترة داخلية بطول كامل

23. half slip
سترة داخلية بنصف طول

24. knee-highs
جورب حتى الركبة

25. kneesocks
جورب تحت الركبة

26. stockings
جوارب فوق الركبة نسائي

27. pantyhose
جورب بنطالي نسائي

More vocabulary

lingerie: underwear or sleepwear for women

loungewear: clothing (sometimes sleepwear) people wear around the home

Share your answers.

1. What do you wear when you exercise?

2. What kind of clothing do you wear for sleeping?

Shoes and Accessories الأحذية والأكسسوارات

1. salesclerk
البائع

2. suspenders
حمالة البنطلون

3. shoe department
قسم الأحذية

4. silk scarves*
وشاح حرير

5. hats
قبعات

12. sole
نعل حذاء

13. heel
كعب

14. shoelace
رباط الحذاء

15. toe
اصبع القدم

16. pumps
حذاء نسائي

17. high heels
حذاء ذو كعب عالي

18. boots
جزمة

19. loafers
حذاء موكاسان

20. oxfords
حذاء اكسفورد

21. hiking boots
حذاء للتسلق

22. tennis shoes
حذاء تنس

23. athletic shoes
حذاء رياضي

24. sandals
صندل

***Note:** one scarf, two scarves*

Talk about the shoes you're wearing today.

I'm wearing a pair of <u>white sandals</u>.

Practice asking a salesperson for help.

Could I try on these <u>sandals</u> in size <u>10</u>?

Do you have any <u>silk scarves</u>?

Where are <u>the hats</u>?

6. purses/handbags حقائب وشنط	**8.** jewelry مجوهرات	**10.** ties رباط عنق
7. display case صندوق نافذة للعرض	**9.** necklaces قلائد	**11.** belts أحزمة

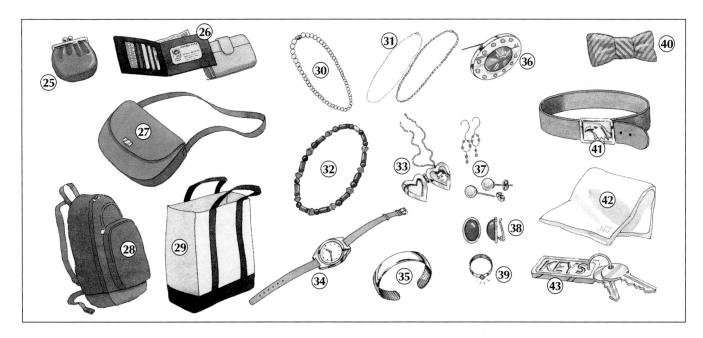

25. change purse كيس نقود	**30.** string of pearls عقد لؤلؤ	**35.** bracelet سوار	**40.** bow tie رباط عنق فراشي الشكل
26. wallet محفظة	**31.** chain سلسلة	**36.** pin دبوس	**41.** belt buckle ابزيم الحزام
27. shoulder bag حقيبة نسائية	**32.** beads خرز	**37.** pierced earrings حلق لأذن مثقوبة	**42.** handkerchief منديل
28. backpack/bookbag حقيبة ظهر	**33.** locket المدلاة	**38.** clip-on earrings حلق بمشبك	**43.** key chain سلسلة مفاتيح
29. tote bag حقيبة نقل	**34.** (wrist)watch ساعة يد	**39.** ring خاتم	

Share your answers.

1. Which of these accessories are usually worn by women? by men?

2. Which of these do you wear every day?

3. Which of these would you wear to a job interview? Why?

4. Which accessory would you like to receive as a present? Why?

Describing Clothes وصف الملابس

Sizes المقاسات

1. extra small
صغير جدا

2. small
صغير

3. medium
متوسط

4. large
كبير

5. extra large
كبير جدا

Patterns أشكال القماش

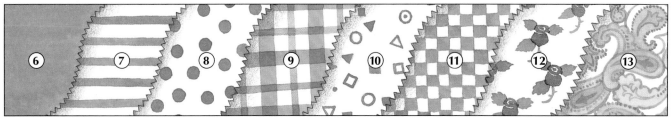

6. solid green
أخضر مصمت

7. striped
مخطط

8. polka-dotted
منقط

9. plaid
مربع

10. print
منقش

11. checked
ذو مربعات

12. floral
ذو أشكال وردية

13. paisley
نسيج صوف مزركش

Types of material أنواع النسيج

14. **wool** sweater
سترة من الصوف

15. **silk** scarf
وشاح من الحرير

16. **cotton** T-shirt
بلوزة من القطن

17. **linen** jacket
جاكيت من الكتان

18. **leather** boots
حذاء جلد عالي الساق/ بوت

19. **nylon** stockings*
جوارب نايلون

Problems المشاكل

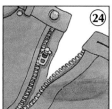
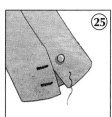

20. too small
صغير جدا

21. too big
كبير جدا

22. stain
بقعة

23. rip/tear
تمزق

24. **broken** zipper
زمام منزلق/ سوستة مكسورة

25. **missing** button
زر مفقود

*Note: Nylon, polyester, rayon, and plastic are synthetic materials.

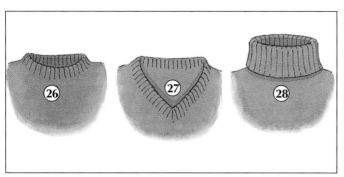

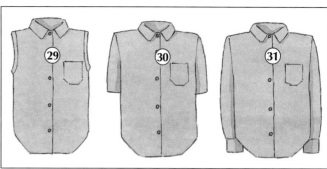

26. crewneck sweater
بلوفر/ كنزة ذو ياقة عالية

27. V-neck sweater
بلوفر/ كنزة ذو ياقة على شكل ٧

28. turtleneck sweater
بلوفر/ كنزة ذو ياقة عالية جدا

29. sleeveless shirt
قميص بدون أكمام

30. short-sleeved shirt
قميص ذو أكمام قصيرة

31. long-sleeved shirt
قميص ذو أكمام طويلة

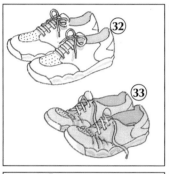

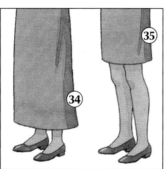

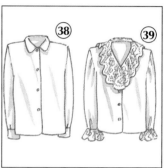

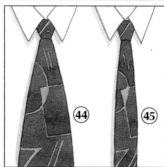

32. new shoes
حذاء جديد

33. old shoes
حذاء قديم

34. long skirt
تنورة طويلة

35. short skirt
تنورة قصيرة

36. formal dress
فستان رسمي

37. casual dress
فستان غير رسمي

38. plain blouse
بلوزة بسيطة

39. fancy blouse
بلوزة مزركشة

40. light jacket
جاكيت خفيف

41. heavy jacket
جاكيت ثقيل

42. loose pants/**baggy** pants
بنطلون فضفاض

43. tight pants
بنطلون ضيق

44. wide tie
ياقة عريضة

45. narrow tie
ياقة رفيعة

46. low heels
كعب واطئ

47. high heels
كعب عالي

Talk about yourself.

I like _long-sleeved_ shirts and _baggy_ pants.

I like _short skirts_ and _high heels_.

I usually wear _plain_ clothes.

Share your answers.

1. What type of material do you usually wear in the summer? in the winter?

2. What patterns do you see around you?

3. Are you wearing casual or formal clothes?

Doing the Laundry غسل الملابس

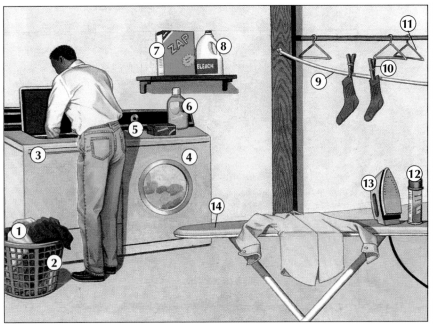

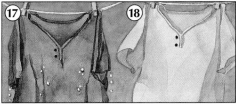
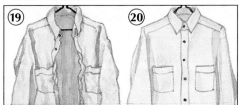

1. **laundry**
   ملابس للغسل
2. **laundry basket**
   سلة ملابس
3. **washer**
   غسالة ملابس
4. **dryer**
   نشافة ملابس
5. **dryer sheets**
   أوراق نشافة

6. **fabric softener**
   مطرّي للنسيج
7. **laundry detergent**
   مسحوق الغسيل
8. **bleach**
   مبيّض
9. **clothesline**
   منشر الغسيل
10. **clothespin**
    مشبك الملابس

11. **hanger**
    حمالة الثياب
12. **spray starch**
    رشاش النشا
13. **iron**
    مكواة
14. **ironing board**
    طاولة الكيّ
15. **dirty** T-shirt
    تي شرت متسخ

16. **clean** T-shirt
    تي شرت نظيف
17. **wet** T-shirt
    تي شرت مبلل
18. **dry** T-shirt
    تي شرت جاف
19. **wrinkled** shirt
    قميص متجعد
20. **ironed** shirt
    قميص مكوي

A. **Sort** the laundry.
   تفرز الغسيل.
B. **Add** the detergent.
   تضيف مسحوق الغسيل.
C. **Load** the washer.
   تضع الغسيل في الغسالة.

D. **Clean** the lint trap.
   تنظف مكان تجمع النسالة.
E. **Unload** the dryer.
   تفرغ مجفف الملابس.
F. **Fold** the laundry.
   تطوي الملابس.

G. **Iron** the clothes.
   تكوي الملابس.
H. **Hang up** the clothes.
   تعلق الملابس.

More vocabulary

dry cleaners: a business that cleans clothes using chemicals, not water and detergent

 wash in cold water only

 no bleach

 line dry

 dry-clean only, do not wash

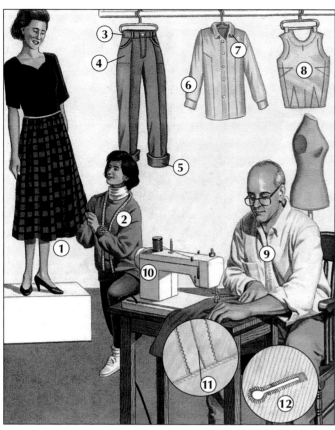

A. **sew** by hand
تخيط باليد

B. **sew** by machine
تخيط بماكينة الخياطة

C. **lengthen**
تطوّل

D. **shorten**
تقصّر

E. **take in**
تضيّق

F. **let out**
توسّع

1. hemline
حاشية
2. dressmaker
خيّاطة
3. waistband
خط الوسط

4. pocket
الجيب
5. cuff
طرف الكم
6. sleeve
الكم

7. collar
قبة
8. pattern
نموذج التفصيل
9. tailor
خيّاط

10. sewing machine
ماكينة الخياطة
11. seam
اللفق/ درز
12. buttonhole
عروة الزر

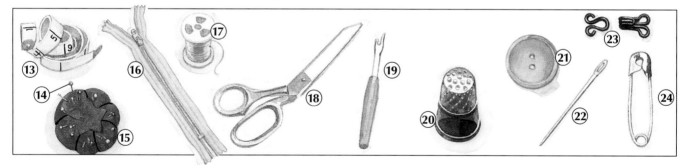

13. tape measure
شريط القياس
14. pin
دبوس
15. pin cushion
حامل الدبابيس/ مدبسة

16. zipper
زمام منزلق/ سوستة
17. spool of thread
بكرة
18. (pair of) scissors
مقص

19. seam ripper
نازع اللفق/ الدرز
20. thimble
كشتبان
21. button
زر

22. needle
إبرة
23. hook and eye
مشبك وفتحة
24. safety pin
دبوس مشبك

More vocabulary

pattern maker: a person who makes patterns

garment worker: a person who works in a clothing factory

fashion designer: a person who makes original clothes

Share your answers.

1. Do you know how to use a sewing machine?
2. Can you sew by hand?

73

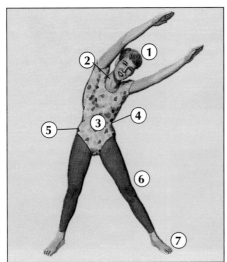

1. head
راس

2. neck
رقبة

3. abdomen
بطن

4. waist
خصر

5. hip
مفصل الورك

6. leg
رجل

7. foot
قدم

8. hand
يد

9. arm
ذراع

10. shoulder
كتف

11. back
ظهر

12. buttocks
الردف

13. chest
صدر

14. breast
ثدي

15. elbow
كوع

16. thigh
فخذ

17. knee
ركبة

18. calf
ربلة أو بطة الساق

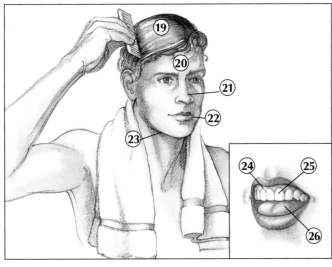

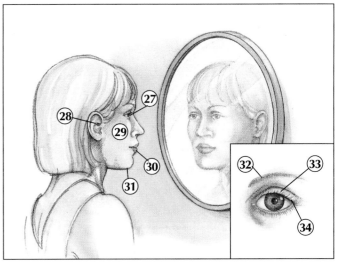

The face
الوجه

19. hair
شعر

20. forehead
جبهة

21. nose
أنف

22. mouth
فم

23. jaw
فك

24. gums
لثة

25. teeth
أسنان

26. tongue
لسان

27. eye
عين

28. ear
أذن

29. cheek
خد

30. lip
شفة

31. chin
ذقن

32. eyebrow
حاجب

33. eyelid
جفن

34. eyelashes
رموش

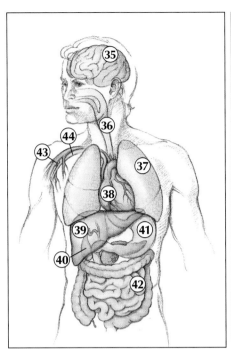

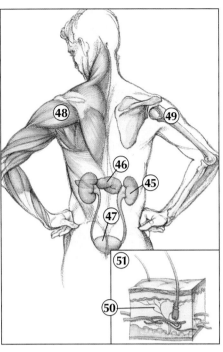

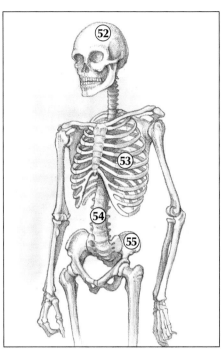

Inside the body
أعضاء الجسم

35. brain
المخ

36. throat
البلعوم

37. lung
الرئة

38. heart
القلب

39. liver
الكبد

40. gallbladder
المرارة

41. stomach
المعدة

42. intestines
الأمعاء

43. artery
الأوعية الدموية

44. vein
العروق

45. kidney
الكلية

46. pancreas
البانكرياس

47. bladder
المثانة

48. muscle
العضل

49. bone
العظم

50. nerve
العصب

51. skin
الجلد

The skeleton
الهيكل العظمي

52. skull
الجمجمة

53. rib cage
القفص الصدري

54. spinal column
العمود الفقري

55. pelvis
الحوض

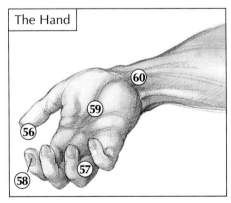

The Hand

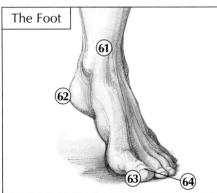

The Foot

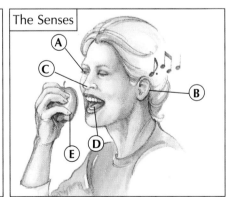

The Senses

56. thumb
الإبهام

57. fingers
الأصابع

58. fingernail
الأظافر

59. palm
الكف

60. wrist
الرسغ

61. ankle
الكاحل

62. heel
الكعب

63. toe
أصبع القدم

64. toenail
أظفر القدم

A. see
يرى

B. hear
يسمع

C. smell
يشم

D. taste
يتذوق

E. touch
يحس

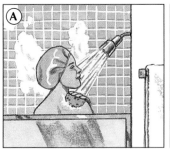   

A. take a shower
تستحم

B. bathe / take a bath
يأخذ حمام

C. use deodorant
يستعمل مزيل رائحة العرق

D. put on sunscreen
تضع مستحضر حاجز للشمس

1. shower cap
غطاء شعر للحمام

2. soap
صابون

3. bath powder / talcum powder
بودرة

4. deodorant
مزيل رائحة العرق

5. perfume / cologne
كولونيا / عطر

6. sunscreen
حاجز الشمس

7. body lotion
كريم للجسم

8. moisturizer
مرطب للجلد

 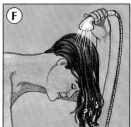   

E. wash…hair
تغسل الشعر

F. rinse…hair
تشطف الشعر

G. comb…hair
تمشط الشعر

H. dry…hair
تجفف الشعر

I. brush…hair
تصفف الشعر بالفرشاة

9. shampoo
شامبو

10. conditioner
منعّم الشعر

11. hair gel
جيل الشعر

12. hair spray
مثبّت شعر

13. comb
مشط

14. brush
فرشاة

15. curling iron
مكواة شعر

16. blow dryer
مجفّف شعر

17. hair clip
دبوس شعر

18. barrette
مشبك شعر

19. bobby pins
دبوس شعر محكم

J. brush...teeth
ينظف الأسنان بالفرشاة

K. floss...teeth
ينظف الأسنان بالخيط

L. gargle
يتغرغر

M. shave
يحلق

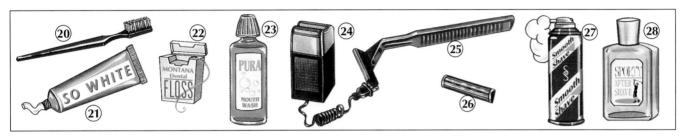

20. toothbrush
فرشاة الأسنان

21. toothpaste
معجون الأسنان

22. dental floss
خيط لتنظيف الأسنان

23. mouthwash
مستحضر لغسل الفم

24. electric shaver
ماكينة حلاقة كهربائية

25. razor
ماكينة حلاقة

26. razor blade
موس حلاقة

27. shaving cream
معجون حلاقة

28. aftershave
كولونيا بعد الحلاقة

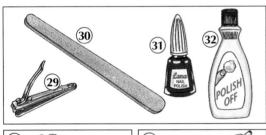

N. cut...nails
تقلم... الأظافر

O. polish...nails
تطلي... الأظافر

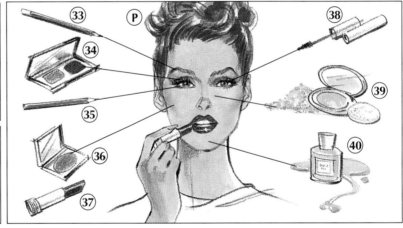

P. put on...makeup
تضع... المكياج

29. nail clipper
مقلمة أظافر

30. emery board
مبرد أظافر

31. nail polish
طلاء الأظافر

32. nail polish remover
مزيل طلاء الأظافر

33. eyebrow pencil
قلم حواجب

34. eye shadow
قلم كحل

35. eyeliner
قلم تخطيط العين

36. blush / rouge
أحمر خدود

37. lipstick
أحمر الشفاه

38. mascara
ماسكرا/ مستحضر تجميلي

39. face powder
بودرة للوجه

40. foundation
كريم أساس

More vocabulary

A product without perfume or scent is **unscented.**

A product that is better for people with allergies is **hypoallergenic.**

Share your answers.

1. What is your morning routine if you stay home? if you go out?

2. Do women in your culture wear makeup? How old are they when they begin to use it?

1. headache صداع	**6.** sore throat التهاب الحنجرة
2. toothache وجع أسنان	**7.** nasal congestion احتقان في الأنف
3. earache ألم في الأذن	**8.** fever / temperature حمى / حرارة
4. stomachache ألم في المعدة	**9.** chills رعشة
5. backache ألم في الظهر	**10.** rash طفح جلدي

A. **cough** يسعل
B. **sneeze** يعطس
C. **feel** dizzy يشعر/ تشعر بالدوران
D. **feel** nauseous تشعر بالغثيان
E. **throw up / vomit** تتقيأ/ يستفرغ – تستفرغ

11. insect bite لسعة حشرة	**14.** sunburn سفعة شمس	**17.** **bloody** nose نزيف في الأنف
12. bruise كدمة	**15.** blister قرحة (كلو)	**18.** **sprained** ankle التواء الكاحل
13. cut جرح	**16.** **swollen** finger ورم في الأصبع	

Use the new language.

Look at **Health Care,** pages 80–81.

Tell what medication or treatment you would use for each health problem.

Share your answers.

1. For which problems would you go to a doctor? use medication? do nothing?

2. What do you do for a sunburn? for a headache?

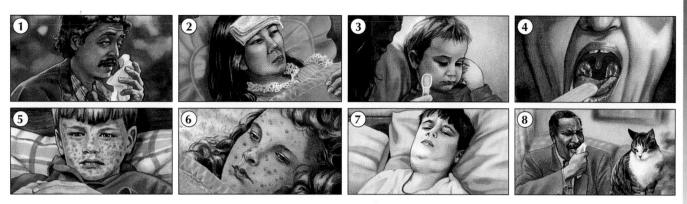

Common illnesses and childhood diseases الأمراض الشائعة، أمراض الطفولة

1. cold
البرد

2. flu
الانفلونزا

3. ear infection
التهاب في الأذن

4. strep throat
التهاب في الحنجرة

5. measles
الحصبة

6. chicken pox
جدري الماء

7. mumps
أبو كعب / النكاف

8. allergies
الحساسية

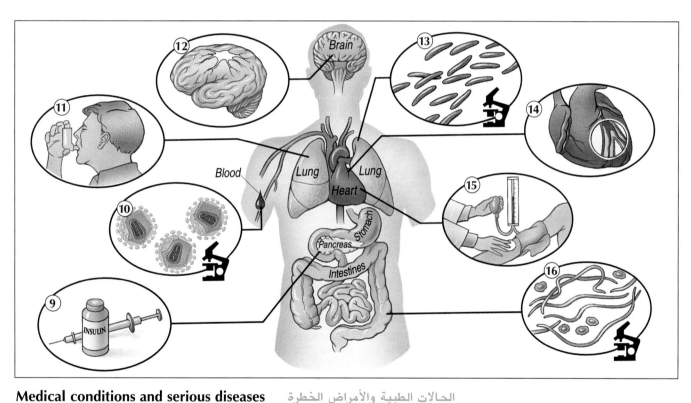

Medical conditions and serious diseases الحالات الطبية والأمراض الخطرة

9. diabetes
مرض السكري

10. HIV (human immunodeficiency virus)
جرثومة نقص المناعة البشرية

11. asthma
الربو

12. brain cancer
سرطان المخ

13. TB (tuberculosis)
السل

14. heart disease
مرض القلب

15. high blood pressure
ضغط دم عالي

16. intestinal parasites
الدود المعوي

More vocabulary

AIDS (acquired immunodeficiency syndrome): a medical condition that results from contracting the HIV virus

influenza: flu

hypertension: high blood pressure

infectious disease: a disease that is spread through air or water

Share your answers.

Which diseases on this page are infectious?

Health Care رعاية صحية

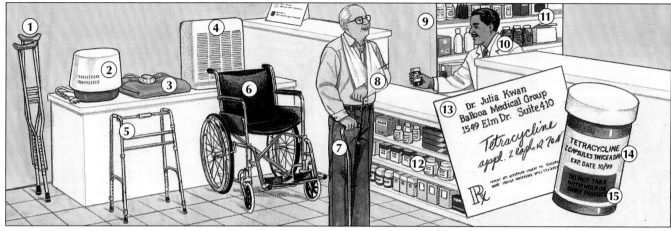

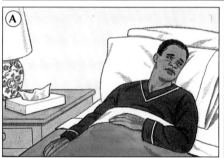

1. crutches
عكاز

2. humidifier
مرطب للهواء

3. heating pad
لبادة تدفئة

4. air purifier
منقي للهواء

5. walker
ممشاة

6. wheelchair
كرسي بعجلات

7. cane
عصا

8. sling
المعلاق

9. pharmacy
صيدلية

10. pharmacist
صيدلي

11. prescription medication
دواء بوصفة طبية / روشته

12. over-the-counter medication
أدوية بدون وصفة طبية

13. prescription
وصفة طبية

14. prescription label
بطاقة وصفة طبية

15. warning label
بطاقة تحذير

A. **Get** bed rest.
الزم الفراش.

B. **Drink** fluids.
أشربي سوائل.

C. **Change** your diet.
غيّر/ ي طعامك.

D. **Exercise.**
مارس/ي رياضة.

E. **Get** an injection.
خذي حقنة.

F. **Take** medicine.
خذ الدواء.

More vocabulary

dosage: how much medicine you take and how many times a day you take it

expiration date: the last day the medicine can be used

treatment: something you do to get better

Staying in bed, drinking fluids, and getting physical therapy are treatments.

An injection that stops a person from getting a serious disease is called **an immunization** or **a vaccination.**

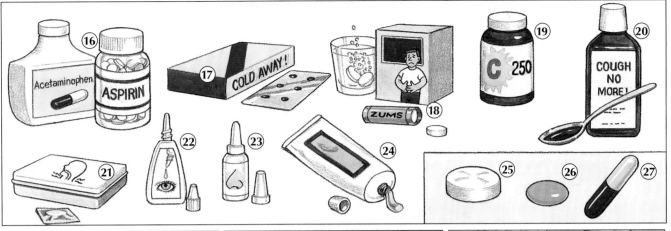

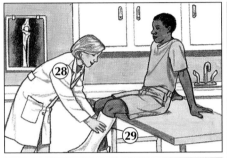

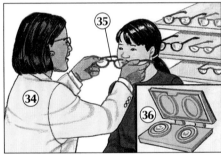

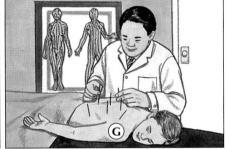

16. pain reliever مسكّن للآلام	**24.** ointment مرهم	**32.** audiologist طبيب أذن
17. cold tablets حبوب للزكام	**25.** tablet قرص	**33.** hearing aid سماعة أذن
18. antacid مضاد للحموضة	**26.** pill حبة	**34.** optometrist طبيب عيون
19. vitamins فيتامينات	**27.** capsule كبسولة	**35.** (eye)glasses نظارات
20. cough syrup دواء سائل للسعال	**28.** orthopedist المجبر	**36.** contact lenses عدسات لاصقة
21. throat lozenges ملطفات للحنجرة	**29.** cast جبص / جبيرة	**G.** **Get** acupuncture. تعالج بالأبر الصينية.
22. eyedrops قطرة للعين	**30.** physical therapist أخصائي علاج طبيعي	**H.** **Go** to a chiropractor. راجع اخصائي في العمود الفقري.
23. nasal spray رشاش للأنف	**31.** brace مقوّم	

Share your answers.

1. What's the best treatment for a headache? a sore throat? a stomachache? a fever?

2. Do you think vitamins are important? Why or why not?

3. What treatments are popular in your culture?

Medical Emergencies حالات طبية طارئة

  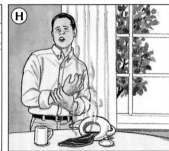

 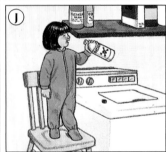 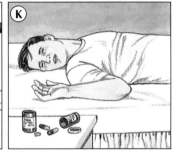 

A. **be injured / be hurt**
يصاب بأذى

B. **be** unconscious
يفقد/ تفقد الوعي

C. **be** in shock
يصاب بصدمة

D. **have** a heart attack
يصاب بنوبة قلبية

E. **have** an allergic reaction
يعاني من حساسية

F. **get** an electric shock
يصاب بصدمة كهربائية

G. **get** frostbite
يقرسه الصقيع

H. **burn** (your)self
يحرق نفسه

I. **drown**
يغرق

J. **swallow** poison
تشرب السم

K. **overdose** on drugs
يتناول كمية مفرطة من الدواء

L. **choke**
تغص

M. **bleed**
ينزف دما

N. **can't breathe**
لم يستطع التنفس

O. **fall**
تقع

P. **break** a bone
يكسر عظمة من عظامه

Grammar point: past tense

burn	—	burned	choke	—	choked	bleed	—	bled
drown	—	drowned	be	—	was, were	can't	—	couldn't
swallow	—	swallowed	have	—	had	fall	—	fell
overdose	—	overdosed	get	—	got	break	—	broke

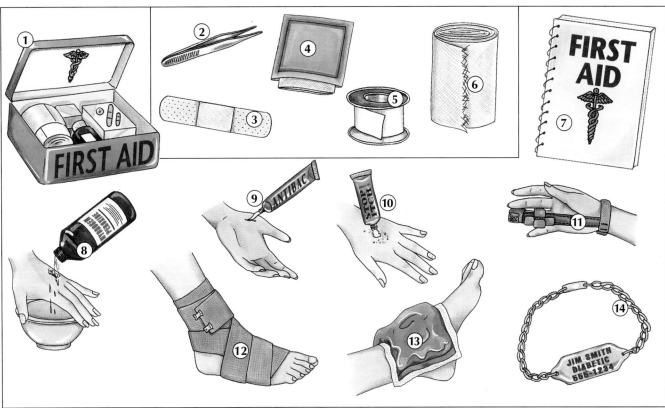

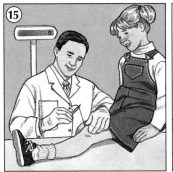

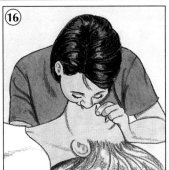

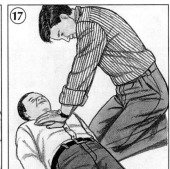

1. first aid kit
مجموعة اسعافات أولية

2. tweezers
ملقط

3. adhesive bandage
ضمادة لاصقة

4. sterile pad
ضمادة معقمة

5. tape
شريط لاصق

6. gauze
شاش

7. first aid manual
كتيب اسعافات أولية

8. hydrogen peroxide
هيدروجين بيروكسيد

9. antibacterial ointment
مرهم مضاد للجراثيم

10. antihistamine cream
كريم مضاد للهستمين

11. splint
جبيرة لليد

12. elastic bandage
ضمادة مطاطية

13. ice pack
حزمة ثلج

14. medical emergency bracelet
سوارة طوارئ طبية

15. stitches
درزة/ غرزة

16. rescue breathing
تنفس انقاذ

17. CPR (cardiopulmonary resuscitation)
انعاش التنفس

18. Heimlich maneuver
طريقة هيمليك لمعالجة الاختناق

Important Note: Only people who are properly trained should give stitches or do CPR.

Share your answers.

1. Do you have a First Aid kit in your home? Where can you buy one?

2. When do you use hydrogen peroxide? an elastic support bandage? antihistamine cream?

3. Do you know first aid? Where did you learn it?

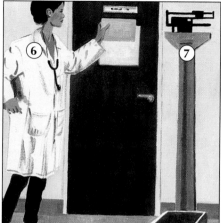

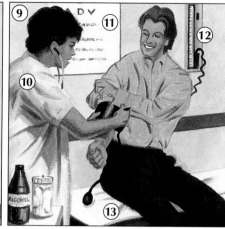

Medical clinic عيادة طبية

1. waiting room
حجرة الانتظار

2. receptionist
موظفة الاستقبال

3. patient
المريض

4. insurance card
بطاقة التأمين الصحي

5. insurance form
استمارة التأمين

6. doctor
دكتور/ طبيب

7. scale
ميزان

8. stethoscope
سماعة طبية

9. examining room
حجرة الكشف

10. nurse
ممرضة

11. eye chart
لوحة اختبار النظر

12. blood pressure gauge
جهاز لقياس ضغط الدم

13. examination table
طاولة الكشف

14. syringe
أبرة/ سرنجة

15. thermometer
مقياس حرارة

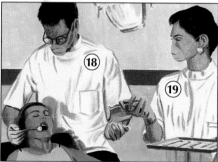
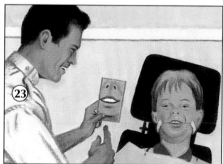
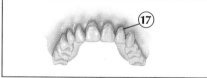
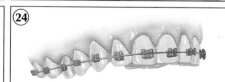

Dental clinic عيادة أسنان

16. dental hygienist
أخصائي صحة أسنان

17. tartar
جير/ القلاح

18. dentist
طبيب أسنان

19. dental assistant
مساعد طبيب أسنان

20. cavity
نخر

21. drill
مثقاب

22. filling
حشو

23. orthodontist
الطبيب مقوّم الأسنان المعوجة

24. braces
مقوّم أسنان

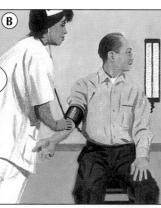

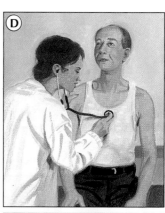

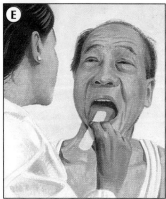

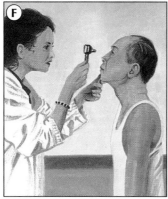

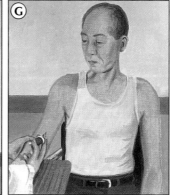

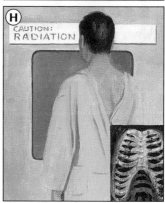

A. make an appointment
تعيِّن موعدا

B. check...blood pressure
تفحص ضغط الدم

C. take...temperature
تفحص درجة الحرارة

D. listen to...heart
تستمع لنبض القلب

E. look in...throat
تنظر إلى الحنجرة

F. examine...eyes
تفحص العينين

G. draw...blood
تسحب الدم

H. get an X ray
يحصل على صورة أشعة اكس

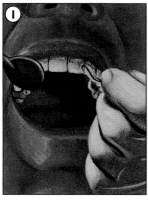

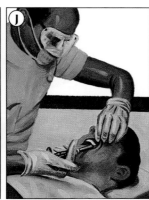

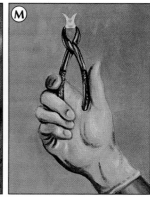

I. clean...teeth
ينظف الأسنان

J. give...a shot of anesthetic
يحقن حقنة تخدير

K. drill a tooth
يحفر السن

L. fill a cavity
يملأ النخر

M. pull a tooth
يقتلع السن

More vocabulary

get a checkup: to go for a medical exam

extract a tooth: to pull out a tooth

Share your answers.

1. What is the average cost of a medical exam in your area?

2. Some people are nervous at the dentist's office. What can they do to relax?

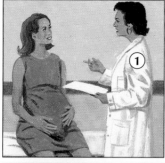

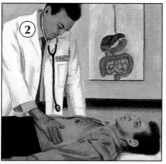

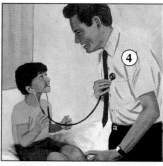
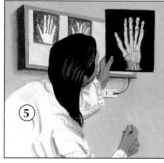
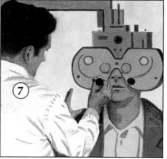
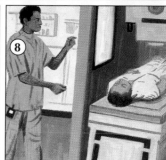

Hospital staff   العاملين بالمستشفى

1. obstetrician
طبيب ولادة

2. internist
طبيب باطني

3. cardiologist
طبيب قلب

4. pediatrician
طبيب أطفال

5. radiologist
طبيب الطاقة الإشعاعية

6. psychiatrist
طبيب أمراض نفسية

7. ophthalmologist
طبيب عيون

8. X-ray technician
أخصائي أشعة اكس

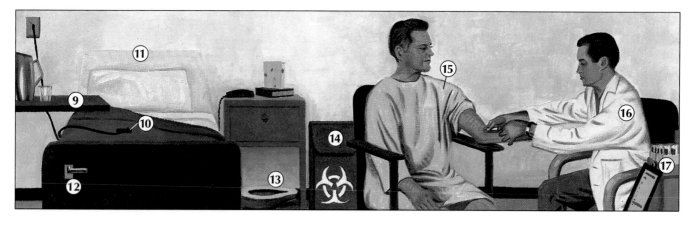

Patient's room   غرفة المريض

9. bed table
طاولة سرير

10. call button
جرس الاستدعاء

11. hospital bed
سرير المستشفى

12. bed control
المتحكم في حركة السرير

13. bedpan
وعاء للسرير/ نونية

14. medical waste disposal
سلة المهملات الطبية

15. hospital gown
رداء المريض

16. lab technician
اخصائي مختبر

17. blood work/blood test
تحليل الدم

More vocabulary

nurse practitioner: a nurse licensed to give medical exams

specialist: a doctor who only treats specific medical problems

gynecologist: a specialist who examines and treats women

nurse midwife: a nurse practitioner who examines pregnant women and delivers babies

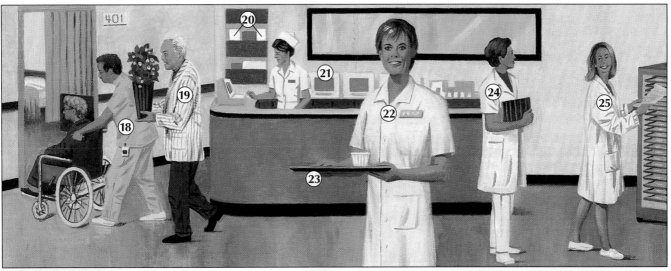

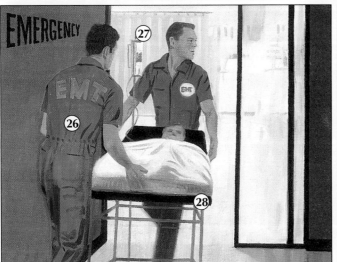

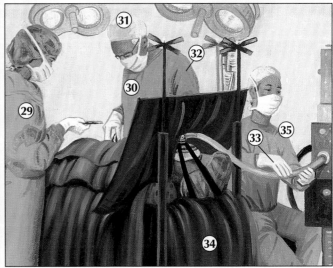

Nurse's station
مركز الممرضات/ الممرضين

18. orderly
ممرض

19. volunteer
متطوع

20. medical charts
بيانات طبية

21. vital signs monitor
مرقاب الذبذبات

22. RN (registered nurse)
ممرضة مؤهلة

23. medication tray
صينية خاصة بالدواء

24. LPN (licensed practical nurse)/ LVN (licensed vocational nurse)
ممرضة ممارسة مؤهلة
ممرضة مهنية مؤهلة

25. dietician
طبيب تغذية

Emergency room
غرفـة الإسـعاف

26. emergency medical technician (EMT)
اخصائي طبي لحالات الطوارئ

27. IV (intravenous drip)
سائل تغذية يعطى في الوريد

28. stretcher/gurney
نقالة مرضى

Operating room
غرفة العمليات

29. surgical nurse
ممرضة جراحة

30. surgeon
جرّاح

31. surgical cap
غطاء رأس لغرفة العمليات

32. surgical gown
رداء غرفة العمليات

33. latex gloves
قفاز مطاطي

34. operating table
طاولة الجراحة

35. anesthesiologist
طبيب التخدير

Practice asking for the hospital staff.

Please get the nurse. I have a question for her.

Where's the anesthesiologist? I need to talk to her.

I'm looking for the lab technician. Have you seen him?

Share your answers.

1. Have you ever been to an emergency room? Who helped you?

2. Have you ever been in the hospital? How long did you stay?

1. fire station
   اطفائية

2. coffee shop
   مقهى

3. bank
   بنك / مصرف

4. car dealership
   معرض سيارات

5. hotel
   فندق

6. church
   كنيسة

7. hospital
   مستشفى

8. park
   منتزه

9. synagogue
   معبد يهودي / كنيس

10. theater
    مسرح

11. movie theater
    دور عرض

12. gas station
    محطة بنزين

13. furniture store
    محل أثاث

14. hardware store
    محل للأدوات المعدنية

15. barber shop
    حلاق

More vocabulary

skyscraper: a very tall office building

downtown / city center: the area in a city with the city hall, courts, and businesses

Practice giving your destination.

I'm going to go downtown.

I have to go to the post office.

16. bakery مخبز	**21.** health club نادي رياضي	**26.** parking garage جراج سيارات/ موقف سيارات
17. city hall مبنى البلدية	**22.** motel موتيل/ فندق صغير	**27.** school مدرسة
18. courthouse محكمة	**23.** mosque جامع	**28.** library مكتبة
19. police station مخفر الشرطة	**24.** office building مبنى خاص للمكاتب	**29.** post office مكتب بريد
20. market سوق	**25.** high-rise building ناطحة سحاب	

Practice asking for and giving the locations of buildings.

Where's <u>the post office</u>?

   It's on <u>Oak Street</u>.

Share your answers.

1. Which of the places in this picture do you go to every week?
2. Is it good to live in a city? Why or why not?
3. What famous cities do you know?

89

1. Laundromat
مغسلة عامة

2. drugstore/pharmacy
صيدلية

3. convenience store
بقالة

4. photo shop
محل تصوير

5. parking space
موقف

6. traffic light
اشارة مرور

7. pedestrian
المشاة

8. crosswalk
ممر المشاة

9. street
شارع

10. curb
حافة الرصيف

11. newsstand
كشك الصحف

12. mailbox
صندوق بريد

13. drive-thru window
نافذة تقديم الأطعمة للسيارات

14. fast food restaurant
مطعم للوجبات السريعة

15. bus
أتوبيس/باص

A. **cross** the street
تعبر الشارع

B. **wait** for the light
ينتظر الإشارة الضوئية

C. **drive** a car
تقود سيارة

More vocabulary

neighborhood: the area close to your home

do errands: to make a short trip from your home to buy
or pick up something

Talk about where to buy things.

You can buy <u>newspapers</u> at <u>a newsstand</u>.

You can buy <u>donuts</u> at <u>a donut shop</u>.

You can buy <u>food</u> at <u>a convenience store</u>.

16. bus stop
موقف أتوبوس/ باص

17. corner
الناصية/ الركن

18. parking meter
عداد موقف السيارة

19. motorcycle
الدراجة البخارية

20. donut shop
محل للكعك المحلي

21. public telephone
تليفون عام

22. copy center/print shop
مطبعة

23. streetlight
عامود الإضاءة

24. dry cleaners
محل للتنظيف الجاف

25. nail salon
محل للعناية بالأظافر

26. sidewalk
الرصيف

27. garbage truck
سيارة النفايات

28. fire hydrant
مطفئة حريق

29. sign
لافتة

30. street vendor
بائع متجول

31. cart
عربة يد

D. **park** the car
يوقف/ توقف السيارة

E. **ride** a bicycle
تركب الدراجة

Share your answers.

1. Do you like to do errands?

2. Do you always like to go to the same stores?

3. Which businesses in the picture are also in your neighborhood?

4. Do you know someone who has a small business? What kind?

5. What things can you buy from a street vendor?

A Mall   مركز تجاري مغلق

1. music store
دكان موسيقى

2. jewelry store
محل بيع المجوهرات

3. candy store
محل بيع الحلوى

4. bookstore
مكتبة

5. toy store
محل لعب

6. pet store
محل للحيوانات الأليفة

7. card store
محل كروت

8. optician
نظاراتي

9. travel agency
مكتب سياحة

10. shoe store
محل أحذية

11. fountain
نافورة

12. florist
بائع الزهور

More vocabulary

beauty shop: hair salon

men's store: a store that sells men's clothing

dress shop: a store that sells women's clothing

Talk about where you want to shop in this mall.

Let's go to the card store.

I need to buy a card for Maggie's birthday.

13. **department store**
محل متعدد الأقسام

14. **food court**
ساحة الطعام

15. **video store**
محل شرائط الفيديو

16. **hair salon**
صالون حلاقة

17. **maternity shop**
محلات بيع ملابس الحوامل

18. **electronics store**
محل أجهزة الكترونية

19. **directory**
الدليل

20. **ice cream stand**
كشك جيلاتي/ بوظة

21. **escalator**
السلم الكهربائي

22. **information booth**
كشك الاستعلامات

Practice asking for and giving the location of different shops.

Where's <u>the maternity shop</u>?

　It's on <u>the first floor</u>, next to <u>the hair salon.</u>

Share your answers.

1. Do you like shopping malls? Why or why not?

2. Some people don't go to the mall to shop.
   Name some other things you can do in a mall.

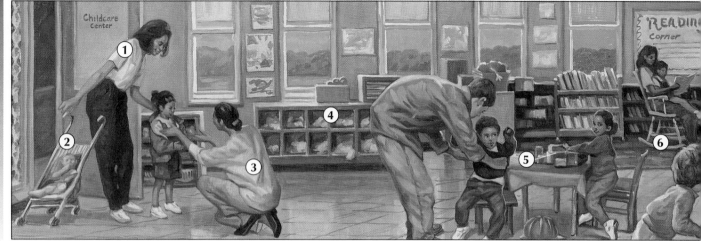

1. parent
والد/ والدة

2. stroller
عربة أطفال

3. childcare worker
اخصائية حضانة الأطفال

4. cubby
غرفة صغيرة

5. toys
لعب

6. rocking chair
كرسي هزّاز

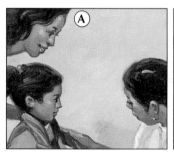

A. **drop off**
توصل

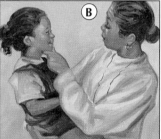

B. **hold**
تحمل

C. **nurse**
تُرضِع

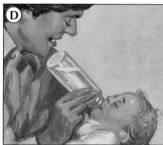

D. **feed**
تطعم

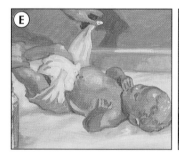

E. **change** diapers
تغيِّر الحفاض

F. **read** a story
تقرأ قصة

G. **pick up**
ترفع

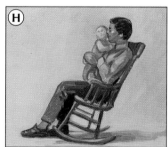

H. **rock**
تهزّ

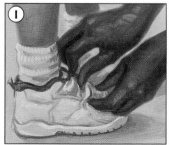

I. **tie** shoes
تربط رباط الحذاء

J. **dress**
تلبس

K. **play**
تلعب

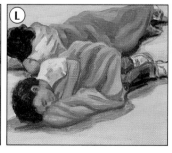

L. **take** a nap
يأخذ/ تأخذ سنه من النوم

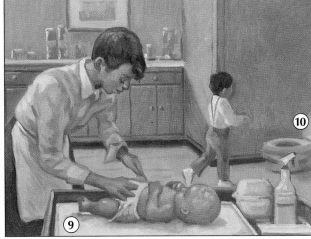

7. high chair
كرسي مرتفع

8. bib
فوطة صدرية

9. changing table
طاولة الغيار

10. potty seat
نونية للأطفال

11. playpen
ملعب نقال للأطفال

12. walker
مشاية

13. car safety seat
كرسي لسلامة الأطفال بالسيارة

14. baby carrier
حمالة أطفال

15. baby backpack
حقيبة لحمل الطفل على الظهر

16. carriage
عربة أطفال

17. wipes
مناديل للتنظيف

18. baby powder
بودرة أطفال

19. disinfectant
مادة مطهَّرة

20. disposable diapers
حفاضات تلقى بعد الاستعمال

21. cloth diapers
حفاضات من القماش

22. diaper pins
دبوس حفاضة

23. diaper pail
سلة الحفاضات

24. training pants
بنطلونات أطفال سهلة الخلع

25. formula
حليب مستحضر

26. bottle
زجاجة رضاعة

27. nipple
حلمة زجاجة الرضاعة

28. baby food
طعام للطفل

29. pacifier
مصَّاصة أطفال

30. teething ring
عضَّاضة

31. rattle
خشخيشة

1. envelope
   مغلف/ ظرف
2. letter
   رسالة
3. postcard
   بطاقة بريدية
4. greeting card
   كارت معايدة
5. package
   طرد

6. letter carrier
   ساعي البريد
7. return address
   عنوان المراسل
8. mailing address
   عنوان المرسل اليه
9. postmark
   ختم البريد
10. stamp/postage
    طابع بريد

11. certified mail
    بريد مسجل
12. priority mail
    بريد مستعجل
13. air letter/aerogramme
    بريد جوي
14. ground post/
    parcel post
    بريد أرضي
15. Express Mail/
    overnight mail
    بريد سريع/ تسليم اليوم التالي

A. **address** a postcard
   يعنون البطاقة البريدية

B. **send** it/**mail** it
   يبعثها/ يرسلها بالبريد

C. **deliver** it
   يسلمها

D. **receive** it
   تستلمها

Emily Rose
1543 Oak Lane
Springvale, CA 91254

SPRINGVALE 5-7-99 CA

USA

Alyson Shepard
249 Courtney Drive
Newton, NY 10043

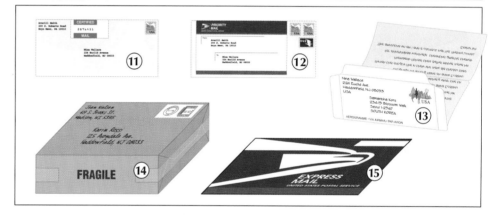

96

1. teller
أمينة الصندوق

2. vault
خزينة

3. ATM (automated teller machine)
جهاز صرف أوتوماتيكي

4. security guard
رجل الأمن

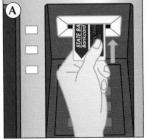

Balance: $235.87

5. passbook
دفتر بنكي

6. savings account number
رقم حساب المدخرات

7. checkbook
دفتر شيكات

8. checking account number
رقم الحساب الجاري

9. ATM card
بطاقة جهاز الصرف الأوتوماتيكي

10. monthly statement
كشف الحساب الشهري

11. balance
الرصيد

12. deposit slip
بيان الايداع

13. safe-deposit box
صندوق حفظ الودائع

Using the ATM machine استعمال آلة الصرف الآلي

A. **Insert** your ATM card.
أدخل بطاقة أى. تي. إم.

B. **Enter** your PIN number.*
أدخل رقمك السري.

C. **Make** a deposit.
أودع نقود أو شيكات.

D. **Withdraw** cash.
يسحب مبلغ نقدي.

E. **Transfer** funds.
يحوّل مبالغ مالية.

F. **Remove** your ATM card.
يسحب بطاقة أي. تي. إم.

*PIN: personal identification number

More vocabulary

overdrawn account: When there is not enough money in an account to pay a check, we say the account is overdrawn.

Share your answers.

1. Do you use a bank?

2. Do you use an ATM card?

3. Name some things you can put in a safe-deposit box.

1. reference librarian أمين المكتبة للمعلومات المرجعية	**7.** magazine مجلة	**13.** videocassette كاسيت فيديو	**19.** library card بطاقة مكتبة
2. reference desk مكتب المعلومات المرجعية	**8.** newspaper صحيفة	**14.** CD (compact disc) اسطوانة مدمجة (سي دي)	**20.** library book كتاب خاص بالمكتبة
3. atlas أطلس	**9.** online catalog كتالوج الكتروني	**15.** record اسطوانة	**21.** title عنوان
4. microfilm reader جهاز المايكروفيلم	**10.** card catalog كتالوج بطاقات الكتب	**16.** checkout desk استعارة الكتب	**22.** author مؤلف
5. microfilm مايكروفيلم	**11.** media section قسم الوسائل الاعلامية	**17.** library clerk كاتب/ موظف	
6. periodical section قسم المنشورات الدورية	**12.** audiocassette كاسيت/ شريط سمعي	**18.** encyclopedia موسوعة	

More vocabulary

check a book out: to borrow a book from the library

nonfiction: real information, history or true stories

fiction: stories from the author's imagination

Share your answers.

1. Do you have a library card?

2. Do you prefer to buy books or borrow them from the library?

A. arrest a suspect
يلقي القبض على مشتبه به

1. police officer
شرطي

2. handcuffs
قيود/ كلبشه

B. hire a lawyer/**hire** an attorney
يعيّن محامي

3. guard
حارس

4. defense attorney
محامي دفاع

C. appear in court
يمثل أمام القضاء

5. defendant
المدعى عليه

6. judge
قاضي

D. stand trial
يخضع للمحاكمة

7. courtroom
محكمة

8. jury
هيئة محلفين

9. evidence
بينة/ دليل

10. prosecuting attorney
النائب العام

11. witness
شاهد

12. court reporter
مراسل محكمة

13. bailiff
حاجب محكمة

E. give the verdict*
يصدر الحكم

F. sentence the defendant
يحكم على المتهم

G. go to jail/**go** to prison
يسجن

14. convict
مدان/ محكوم

H. be released
يفرج عنه

*****Note:** There are two possible verdicts, "guilty" and "not guilty."

Share your answers.

1. What are some differences between the legal system in the United States and the one in your country?

2. Do you want to be on a jury? Why or why not?

Crime جريمـة

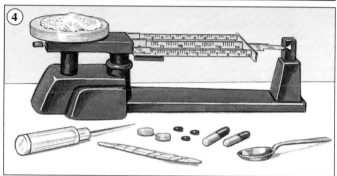

1. vandalism
تخريب متعمد

2. gang violence
عنف عصابات

3. drunk driving
السواقة تحت تأثير الخمر

4. illegal drugs
مخدرات ممنوعة

5. mugging
الاعتداء بهدف السلب

6. burglary
سطو

7. assault
اعتداء

8. murder
جريمة القتل

9. gun
مسدس

More vocabulary

commit a crime: to do something illegal

criminal: someone who commits a crime

victim: someone who is hurt or killed by someone else

Share your answers.

1. Is there too much crime on TV? in the movies?

2. Do you think people become criminals from watching crime on TV?

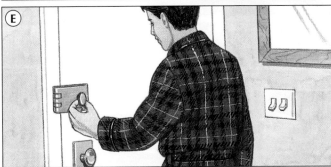

A. **Walk** with a friend.
امش مع صديق/ـة.

B. **Stay** on well-lit streets.
ابق في شوارع جيدة الاضاءة.

C. **Hold** your purse close to your body.
احتفظي بحقيبتك قريبة من جسمك.

D. **Protect** your wallet.
حافظ على حافظة نقودك.

E. **Lock** your doors.
اقفل أبوابك.

F. **Don't open** your door to strangers.
لا تفتح بابك للغرباء.

G. **Don't drink** and **drive**.
لا تشرب الخمر وتسوق.

H. **Report** crimes to the police.
أبلغ الشرطة عن الجرائم.

More vocabulary

Neighborhood Watch: a group of neighbors who watch for criminals in their neighborhood

designated drivers: people who don't drink alcoholic beverages so that they can drive drinkers home

Share your answers.

1. Do you feel safe in your neighborhood?
2. Look at the pictures. Which of these things do you do?
3. What other things do you do to stay safe?

1. lost child
طفل ضائع

2. car accident
حادث طرق

3. airplane crash
تحطم طائرة

4. explosion
انفجار

5. earthquake
هزة أرضية

6. mudslide
انزلاق الطين

7. fire
نار

8. firefighter
اطفائي

9. fire truck
سيارة اطفاء

Practice reporting a fire.

This is <u>Lisa Broad</u>. There is a fire.

The address is <u>323 Oak Street.</u>

Please send someone quickly.

Share your answers.

1. Can you give directions to your home if there is a fire?

2. What information do you give to the other driver if you are in a car accident?

10. drought
جفاف/ قحط

11. blizzard
عاصفة ثلجية

12. hurricane
إعصار

13. tornado
زوبعة

14. volcanic eruption
تفجر البركان

15. tidal wave
موجة بحرية مدية

16. flood
طوفان

17. search and rescue team
فريق البحث والانقاذ

Share your answers.

1. Which disasters are common in your area?
   Which never happen?

2. What can you do to prepare for emergencies?

3. Do you have emergency numbers near your
   telephone?

4. What organizations will help you in an emergency?

Public Transportation النقـل العـام

1. bus stop
موقف أتوبيس/ باص

2. route
طريق

3. schedule
جدول

4. bus
أتوبيس/ باص

5. fare
تعريفة أجرة

6. transfer
تحويل

7. passenger
راكب

8. bus driver
سائق الأتوبيس/ الباص

9. subway
القطار النفقي

10. track
سكة

11. token
عملة رمزية

12. fare card
بطاقة سفر

13. train station
محطة قطار

14. ticket
تذكرة

15. platform
رصيف في محطة القطار

16. conductor
قاطع التذاكر

17. train
قطار

18. taxi/cab
سيارة أجرة/ تاكسي

19. taxi stand
موقف سيارات أجرة

20. taxi driver
سائق سيارة أجرة/ تاكسي

21. meter
عدّاد

22. taxi license
رخصة تاكسي

23. ferry
مركب عبور

More vocabulary

hail a taxi: to get a taxi driver's attention by raising
your hand

miss the bus: to arrive at the bus stop late

Talk about how you and your friends come to school.

I take the bus to school.

You take the train.

We take the subway.

He drives to school.

She walks to school.

They ride bikes.

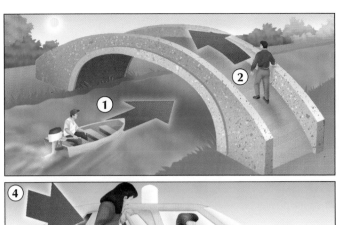

1. **under** the bridge
تحت الجسر
2. **over** the bridge
فوق الجسر
3. **across** the water
عبر الماء
4. **into** the taxi
داخل التاكسي

5. **out of** the taxi
خارج التاكسي
6. **onto** the highway
دخول الطريق العام
7. **off** the highway
الخروج من الطريق العام
8. **down** the stairs
نزول السلم/ الدرج

9. **up** the stairs
صعود السلم/ الدرج
10. **around** the corner
حول المنعطف
11. **through** the tunnel
عبر النفق

Grammar point: *into, out of, on, off*

We say, *get **into** a taxi or a car.*
But we say, *get **on** a bus, a train, or a plane.*

We say, *get **out of** a taxi or a car.*
But we say, *get **off** a bus, a train, or a plane.*

1. subcompact
سيارة اقتصادية صغيرة

2. compact
سيارة صغيرة

3. midsize car
سيارة متوسطة الحجم

4. full-size car
سيارة بحجم كامل

5. convertible
سيارة مكشوفة

6. sports car
سيارة سبور

7. pickup truck
بيك أب

8. station wagon
ستايشن

9. SUV (sports utility vehicle)
سيارة جيب

10. minivan
ميني فان

11. camper
كارافان

12. dump truck
شاحنة النفايات

13. tow truck
سيارة قطر او سحب

14. moving van
سيارة نقل

15. tractor trailer/semi
مقطورة شحن

16. cab
كابينة المقطورة

17. trailer
عربة مقطورة

More vocabulary

make: the name of the company that makes the car

model: the style of car

Share your answers.

1. What is your favorite kind of car?

2. What kind of car is good for a big family? for a single person?

Directions الاتجاهات

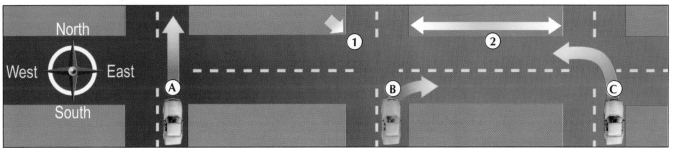

A. go straight
امش باتجاه مستقيم

B. turn right
اتجه/اتجهي إلى اليمين

C. turn left
اتجه/ اتجهي إلى اليسار

1. corner
منعطف

2. block
صف من البيوت أو المحلات

Signs الاشارات

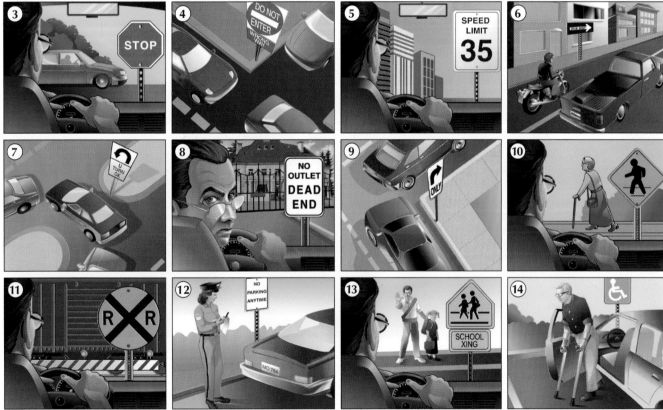

3. stop
توقف/ توقفي

4. do not enter/wrong way
ممنوع الدخول/ طريق خطأ

5. speed limit
السرعة القصوى

6. one way
اتجاه واحد

7. U-turn OK
مسموح الدوران

8. no outlet/dead end
بدون منفذ/ مسدود

9. right turn only
الانعطاف إلى اليمين فقط

10. pedestrian crossing
عبور المشاة

11. railroad crossing
عبور سكة

12. no parking
ممنوع الوقوف

13. school crossing
عبور للمدرسة

14. handicapped parking
موقف للمعاقين

More vocabulary

right-of-way: the right to go first

yield: to give another person or car the right-of-way

Share your answers.

1. Which traffic signs are the same in your country?

2. Do pedestrians have the right-of-way in your city?

3. What is the speed limit in front of your school? your home?

Parts of a Car and Car Maintenance قطع غيار وصيانة السيارات

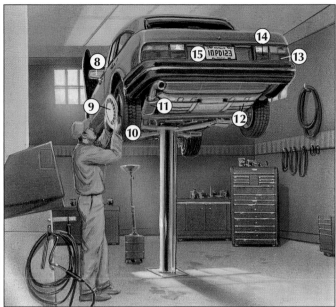

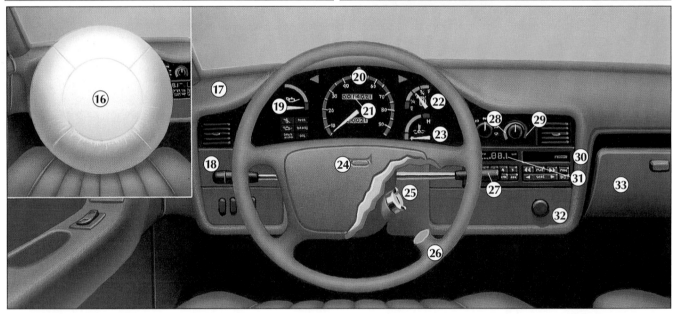

1. rearview mirror مرآة للرؤية الخلفية	**10. tire** عجلة	**19. oil gauge** مقياس الزيت	**28. air conditioning** مكيِّف هوائي
2. windshield حاجب الريح الزجاجي	**11. muffler** مخمد الصوت	**20. speedometer** عداد السرعة	**29. heater** مدفئة
3. windshield wipers المسّاحات	**12. gas tank** خزان البنزين	**21. odometer** أودومتر (عداد المسافة)	**30. tape deck** مسجِّل أشرطة
4. turn signal اشارة تغيير الاتجاه	**13. brake light** مصباح الفرملة	**22. gas gauge** مقياس البنزين	**31. radio** راديو
5. headlight مصباح أمامي	**14. taillight** مصباح خلفي	**23. temperature gauge** مقياس الحرارة	**32. cigarette lighter** ولاعة سجائر
6. hood غطاء محرك السيارة	**15. license plate** لوحة رقم السيارة	**24. horn** بوق	**33. glove compartment** صندوق القفاز
7. bumper مخفف الصدمة	**16. air bag** كيس هوائي	**25. ignition** اشعال	
8. sideview mirror مرآة الرؤية الجانبية	**17. dashboard** تابلو السيارة	**26. steering wheel** عجلة القيادة	
9. hubcap غطاء محور العجلة	**18. turn signal** إشارة الانعطاف	**27. gearshift** ناقل السرعة	

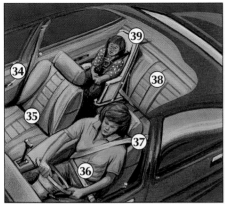

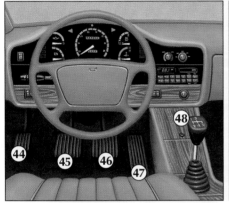

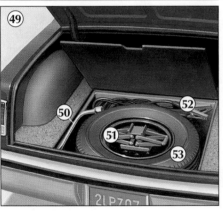

34. lock
قفل

35. front seat
مقعد أمامي

36. seat belt
حزام المقعد

37. shoulder harness
حزام الكتف

38. backseat
مقعد خلفي

39. child safety seat
مقعد أمان للطفل

40. fuel injection system
نظام حقن الوقود

41. engine
محرك

42. radiator
رادياتور (مشعاع)

43. battery
بطارية

44. emergency brake
مكبح للطوارئ

45. clutch*
القابض/ الدوبرياج

46. brake pedal
دواسة المكبح

47. accelerator/gas pedal
دواسة بنزين

48. stick shift
ناقل الحركة

49. trunk
صندوق السيارة

50. lug wrench
مفتاح الربط

51. jack
مرفاع

52. jumper cables
كبل عبور الطاقة

53. spare tire
اطار احتياطي

54. The car needs **gas**.
السيارة بحاجة إلى البنزين.

55. The car needs **oil**.
السيارة بحاجة إلى الزيت.

56. The radiator needs **coolant**.
الرادياتور (المشعاع) بحاجة إلى تبريد.

57. The car needs **a smog check**.
السيارة بحاجة لفحص الغازات الملوثة.

58. The battery needs **recharging**.
البطارية تحتاج إلى إعادة الشحن.

59. The tires need **air**.
الاطارات بحاجة إلى النفخ.

*Note: Standard transmission cars have a clutch; automatic transmission cars do not.

1. airline terminal
صالة المطار

2. airline representative
موظف شركة الطيران

3. check-in counter
مكتب التسجيل

4. arrival and departure monitors
شاشات الوصول والمغادرة

5. gate
بوابة

6. boarding area
منطقة دخول الطائرة

7. control tower
برج المراقبة

8. helicopter
حوامة (هليكوبتر)

9. airplane
طائرة

10. overhead compartment
حجيرة الحقائب المحمولة

11. cockpit
ركن الطيار

12. pilot
طيار

13. flight attendant
مضيف/ مضيفة طائرة

14. oxygen mask
قناع أكسجين

15. airsickness bag
كيس للمصاب بدوار الجو

16. tray table
صينية حاملة

17. baggage claim area
منطقة استرداد الأمتعة

18. carousel
سير الأمتعة المتحرك

19. luggage carrier
عربة أمتعة

20. customs
جمارك

21. customs officer
موظف جمارك

22. declaration form
قسيمة تصريح

23. passenger
مسافر

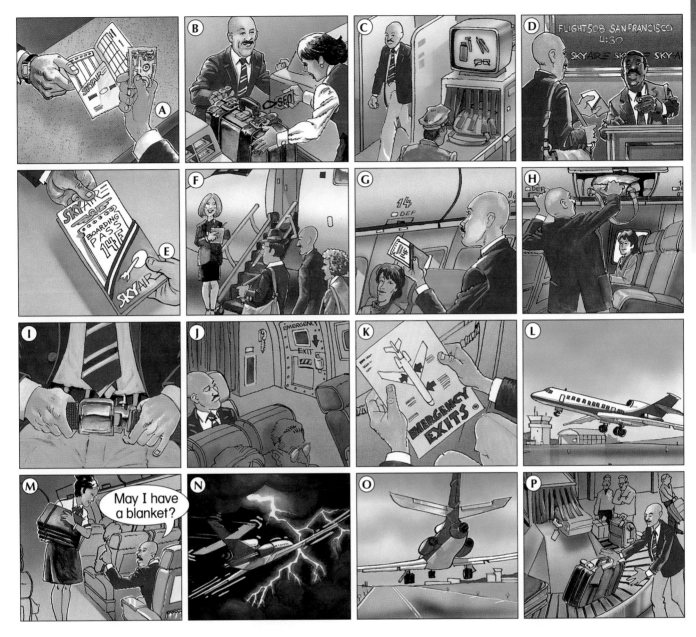

A. **buy** your ticket
يشتري تذكرة

B. **check** your bags
يسلم الحقائب

C. **go through** security
يعبر نقطة الأمن

D. **check in** at the gate
يسلم التذكرة عند البوابة

E. **get** your boarding pass
يحصل على بطاقة الدخول

F. **board** the plane
يدخل الطائرة

G. **find** your seat
يبحث عن مقعده

H. **stow** your carry-on bag
يضع حقائب اليد في المقصورة

I. **fasten** your seat belt
يضع حزام الأمان

J. **look for** the emergency exit
يبحث عن مخرج الطوارئ

K. **look at** the emergency card
ينظر إلى نشرة الطوارئ

L. **take off / leave**
تقلع / تغادر

M. **request** a blanket
يطلب بطانية

N. **experience** turbulence
تمر باضطراب جوي

O. **land / arrive**
تهبط / تصل

P. **claim** your baggage
يسترد الأمتعة

More vocabulary

destination: the place the passenger is going

departure time: the time the plane takes off

arrival time: the time the plane lands

direct flight: a plane trip between two cities with no stops

stopover: a stop before reaching the destination, sometimes to change planes

1. public school
مدرسة حكومية

2. private school
مدرسة خاصة

3. parochial school
مدرسة أبرشية دينية

4. preschool
حضانة

5. elementary school
مدرسة ابتدائية

6. middle school/
junior high school
مدرسة الأحداث العالية/
متوسطة

7. high school
مدرسة ثانوية

8. adult school
مدرسة للكبار

9. vocational school/trade school
مدرسة حرفية مهنية

10. college/university
كلية/جامعة

Note: In the U.S. most children begin school at age 5 (in kindergarten)
and graduate from high school at 17 or 18.

More vocabulary

When students graduate from a college or university
they receive a **degree:**

Bachelor's degree — usually 4 years of study

Master's degree — an additional 1–3 years of study

Doctorate — an additional 3–5 years of study

community college: a two-year college where students
can get an Associate of Arts degree.

graduate school: a school in a university where students
study for their master's and doctorates.

1. writing assignment
فرض كتابي

A. Write a first draft.
أكتب المسودة الأولى.

B. Edit your paper.
نقِح كتابتك.

C. Get feedback.
احصل على رأي شخص آخر.

D. Rewrite your paper.
أعد كتابة موضوعك.

E. Turn in your paper.
سلم موضوعك.

2. paper / composition
موضوع إنشاء

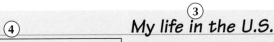

My life in the U.S.

④ I arrived in this country in 1996. My family did not come with me. I was homesick, nervous, and a little excited. I had no job and no friends here. I lived with my aunt and my daily routine ⑤ was always the same: get up, look for a job, go to bed. At night I remembered my mother's words to me, "Son, you can always come home!" I was homesick and scared, but I did not go home.

I started to study English at night. English is a difficult language and many times I was too tired to study. One teacher, Mrs. Armstrong, was very kind to me. She showed me many

3. title
عنوان

4. sentence
جملة

5. paragraph
فقرة

Punctuation علامات تشكيل

6. period
نقطة

7. question mark
علامة استفهام

8. exclamation mark
علامة تعجُب

9. quotation marks
علامتا الاقتباس

10. comma
فاصلة

11. apostrophe
الفاصلة العليا

12. colon
علامة الترقيم

13. semicolon
علامة وقف

113

Exploration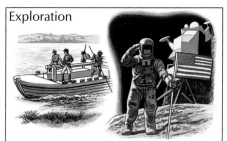

War

Immigration

Historical and Political Events	1492 →	1607–1750	1619 1st African slave sold in Virginia
أحداث تاريخية وسياسية	French, Spanish, English explorers	Colonies along Atlantic coast founded by Northern Europeans	تم بيع أول عبد أفريقي في فرجينيا
	المستكشفين الفرنسيين والاسبانيين والانجليز	مستعمرات على امتداد الساحل الأطلنطي أسّسها الأوربيون الشماليون	1653 1st Indian reservation in Virginia أول أرض مخصصة للهنود في فرجينيا

Before 1700   **1700**

Immigration*	1607	1610
الهجرة	1st English in Virginia أول انجليزي في فرجينيا	Spanish at Santa Fe أسباني في سانتا في

Population**	Before 1700: Native American: 1,000,000+	1700: colonists: 250,000
تعداد السكان**	قبل ١٧٠٠: أمريكيين أصليين: أكثر من مليون	١٧٠٠: المستعمرون: ٢٥٠ ألف

1803	1812	1820	1830	1835–1838	1846–1848
Louisiana Purchase	War of 1812	Missouri Compromise	Indian Removal Act	Cherokee Trail of Tears	U.S. war with Mexico
شراء لويزيانا	حرب ١٨١٢	تسوية ميزوري	قانون ترحيل الهنود	قافلة الدموع – تشيروكي	حرب الولايات المتحدة مع المكسيك

1800   1810   1820   1830   1840

1815 →
Irish
الايرلنديين

1800: citizens and free blacks: 5,300,000   slaves: 450,000
١٨٠٠: المواطنين والسود الأحرار: ٥,٣٠٠,٠٠٠   عبيد: ٤٥٠,٠٠٠

1903	1927	1929	1939–1945	1945
1st Model A Ford car	1st sound pictures	stock market crashes	World War II	United Nations
أول طراز لسيارة فورد	أول أفلام سينمائية ناطقة	تدهور البورصة	الحرب العالمية الثانية	الأمم المتحدة

1st air flight	1914–1918	1920	1930–1940	1945	1948–1985
أول رحلة جوية	World War I	women get vote	The Depression	1st atomic bomb	The Cold War
	الحرب العالمية الأولى	حق التصويت للنساء	الكساد الاقتصادي	أول قنبلة ذرية	الحرب الباردة

1900   1910   1920   1930   1940

1910 →	1924	1942–1945	1945 →	1948
Mexicans	U.S. closes borders	Japanese internment	Puerto Ricans	WW II refugees immigrate
المكسيكيين	الولايات المتحدة تغلق حدودها	اعتقال اليابانيين	البورتريكيين	هجرة لاجئي الحرب العالمية الثانية

1900: 75,994,000

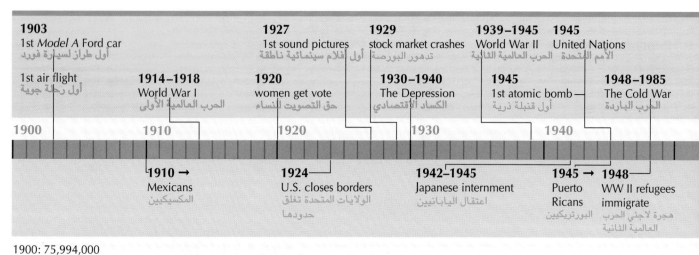

*Immigration dates indicate a time when large numbers of that group first began to immigrate to the U.S.
**All population figures before 1790 are estimates. Figures after 1790 are based on the official U.S. census.

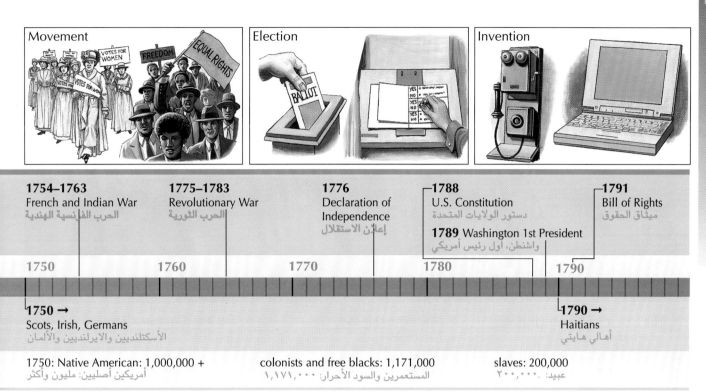

Movement

Election

Invention

1754–1763
French and Indian War
الحرب الفرنسية الهندية

1775–1783
Revolutionary War
الحرب الثورية

1776
Declaration of Independence
إعلان الاستقلال

1788
U.S. Constitution
دستور الولايات المتحدة

1789 Washington 1st President
واشنطن، أول رئيس أمريكي

1791
Bill of Rights
ميثاق الحقوق

1750   1760   1770   1780   1790

1750 →
Scots, Irish, Germans
الأسكتلنديين والايرلنديين والألمان

1790 →
Haitians
أهالي هايتي

1750: Native American: 1,000,000 +
أمريكين أصليين: مليون وأكثر

colonists and free blacks: 1,171,000
المستعمرين والسود الأحرار: ١,١٧١,٠٠٠

slaves: 200,000
عبيد: ٢٠٠,٠٠٠.

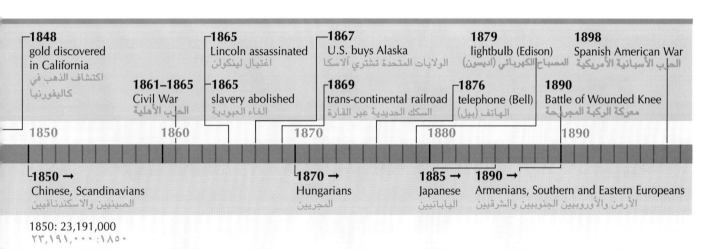

1848
gold discovered in California
اكتشاف الذهب في كاليفورنيا

1861–1865
Civil War
الحرب الأهلية

1865
Lincoln assassinated
اغتيال لينكولن

1865
slavery abolished
الغاء العبودية

1867
U.S. buys Alaska
الولايات المتحدة تشتري ألاسكا

1869
trans-continental railroad
السكك الحديدية عبر القارة

1879
lightbulb (Edison)
المصباح الكهربائي (أديسون)

1876
telephone (Bell)
الهاتف (بيل)

1898
Spanish American War
الحرب الأسبانية الأمريكية

1890
Battle of Wounded Knee
معركة الركبة المجروحة

1850   1860   1870   1880   1890

1850 →
Chinese, Scandinavians
الصينيين والاسكندنافيين

1870 →
Hungarians
المجريين

1885 →
Japanese
اليابانيين

1890 →
Armenians, Southern and Eastern Europeans
الأرمن والأوروبيين الجنوبيين والشرقيين

1850: 23,191,000
١٨٥٠: ٢٣,١٩١,٠٠٠

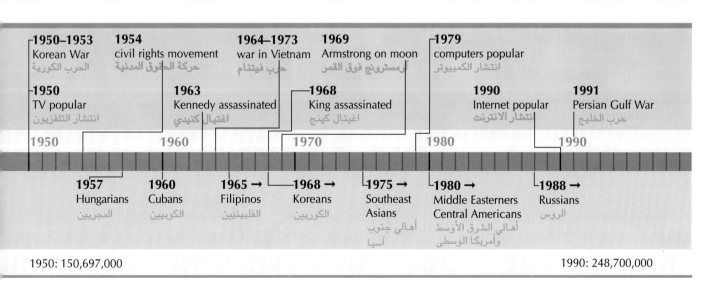

1950–1953
Korean War
الحرب الكورية

1954
civil rights movement
حركة الحقوق المدنية

1964–1973
war in Vietnam
حرب فيتنام

1969
Armstrong on moon
أرمسترونج فوق القمر

1979
computers popular
انتشار الكمبيوتر

1950
TV popular
انتشار التلفزيون

1963
Kennedy assassinated
اغتيال كينيدي

1968
King assassinated
اغتيال كينج

1990
Internet popular
انتشار الانترنت

1991
Persian Gulf War
حرب الخليج

1950   1960   1970   1980   1990

1957
Hungarians
المجريين

1960
Cubans
الكوبيين

1965 →
Filipinos
الفلبينيين

1968 →
Koreans
الكوريين

1975 →
Southeast Asians
أهالي جنوب آسيا

1980 →
Middle Easterners Central Americans
أهالي الشرق الأوسط وأمريكا الوسطى

1988 →
Russians
الروس

1950: 150,697,000

1990: 248,700,000

BRANCHES OF GOVERNMENT

Legislative | Executive | Judicial

1. The House of Representatives
مجلس النواب

2. congresswoman/congressman
عضو أو عضوة كونجرس

3. The Senate
مجلس الشيوخ

4. senator
عضو مجلس الشيوخ

5. The White House
البيت الأبيض

6. president
الرئيس

7. vice president
نائب الرئيس

8. The Supreme Court
المحكمة العليا

9. chief justice
رئيس القضاة

10. justices
قضاة

Citizenship application requirements
شروط الحصول على الجنسية

A. **be** 18 years old
أن يكون عمره ١٨ عاما

B. **live** in the U.S. for five years
أن يكون مقيما في الولايات المتحدة ٥ سنوات

C. **take** a citizenship test
أن يتقدم لامتحان الجنسية

Rights and responsibilities
الحقوق والواجبات

D. **vote**
يصوت/ تصوت

E. **pay** taxes
يدفع الضرائب

F. **register** with Selective Service*
يتسجّل في الخدمة العسكرية

G. **serve** on a jury
يؤدي خدمة هيئة المحلفين

H. **obey** the law
يحترم القانون

*Note: All males 18 to 26 who live in the U.S. are required to register with Selective Service.

1. rain forest
غابات المطر

2. waterfall
شلال ماء

3. river
نهر

4. desert
صحراء

5. sand dune
كثيب

6. ocean
محيط

7. peninsula
شبه جزيرة

8. island
جزيرة

9. bay
خليج

10. beach
شاطئ رملي

11. forest
غابة

12. shore
ساحل

13. lake
بحيرة

14. mountain peak
قمة جبل

15. mountain range
سلسلة جبال

16. hills
تلال

17. canyon
وادي ضيق

18. valley
وادي

19. plains
سهول

20. meadow
مروج

21. pond
بركة

More vocabulary

a body of water: a river, lake, or ocean
stream/creek: a very small river

Talk about where you live and where you like to go.

I live in a valley. There is a lake nearby.
I like to go to the beach.

Mathematics رياضيات

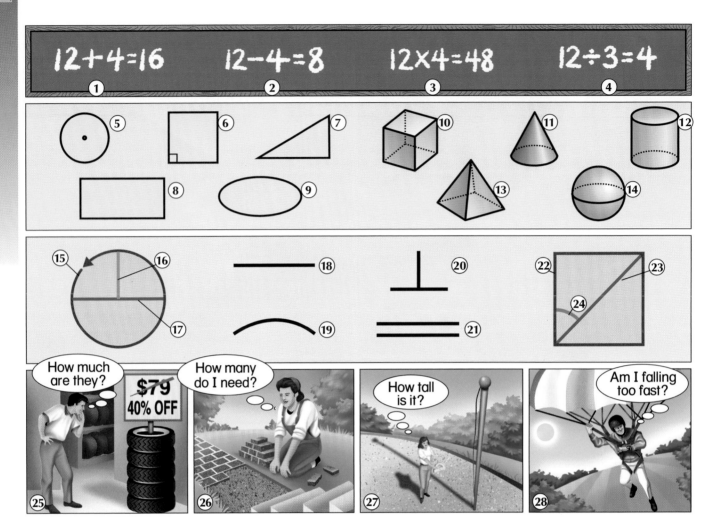

Operations
عمليات حسابية
1. addition
جمع
2. subtraction
طرح
3. multiplication
ضرب
4. division
تقسيم

Shapes
الأشكال
5. circle
دائرة
6. square
مربع
7. triangle
مثلث

8. rectangle
مستطيل
9. oval/ellipse
بيضوي

Solids
أشكال مجسمة
10. cube
مكعب
11. cone
مخروط
12. cylinder
أسطوانة
13. pyramid
هرم
14. sphere
كروي

Parts of a circle
أجزاء دائرة
15. circumference
محيط
16. radius
نصف القطر
17. diameter
القطر

Lines
الخطوط
18. straight
مستقيم
19. curved
منحني
20. perpendicular
متعامد
21. parallel
متوازي

Parts of a square
أجزاء مربع
22. side
ضلع
23. diagonal
وتر
24. angle
زاوية

Types of math
أنواع الرياضيات
25. algebra
الجبر
26. geometry
الهندسة
27. trigonometry
المثلثات
28. calculus
التفاضل والتكامل

More vocabulary

total: the answer to an addition problem

difference: the answer to a subtraction problem

product: the answer to a multiplication problem

quotient: the answer to a division problem

pi (π): the number when you divide the circumference of a circle by its diameter (approximately = 3.14)

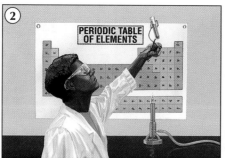

PERIODIC TABLE
OF ELEMENTS

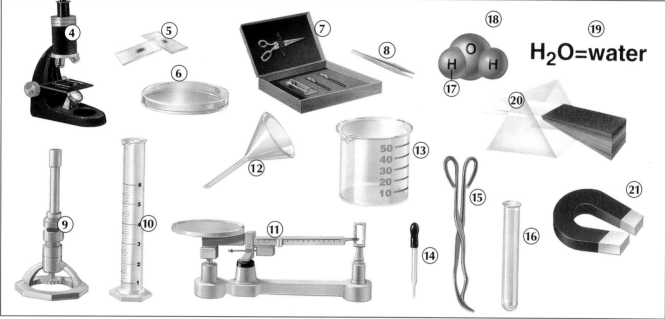

H_2O=water

1. biology
   علم الأحياء

2. chemistry
   الكيمياء

3. physics
   الفيزياء

4. microscope
   مجهر

5. slide
   زجاجة توضع عليها العيّنة

6. petri dish
   صحفة بتري

7. dissection kit
   عدة تشريح

8. forceps
   كلّاب

9. Bunsen burner
   مصباح بنزن

10. graduated cylinder
    أنبوب مدرج

11. balance
    ميزان

12. funnel
    قمع

13. beaker
    كوب صيدلي

14. dropper
    قطارة

15. crucible tongs
    ملقط بوتقي

16. test tube
    أنبوب اختبار

17. atom
    ذرة

18. molecule
    جزيئي

19. formula
    معادلة

20. prism
    موشور

21. magnet
    مغنطيس

A. **do** an experiment
   يقوم بتجربة

B. **observe**
   يلاحظ

C. **record** results
   يسجل النتائج

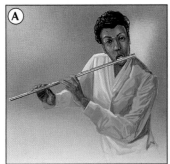

A. play an instrument
يعزف على آلة موسيقية

B. sing a song
يغني أغنية

1. orchestra
أوركسترا

2. rock band
فرقة عزف موسيقى الروك

Woodwinds

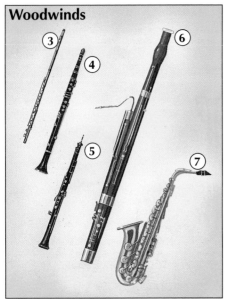

Strings

Brass

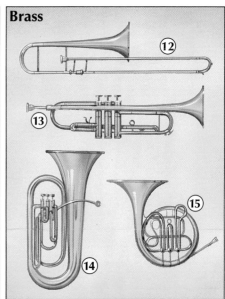

Percussion

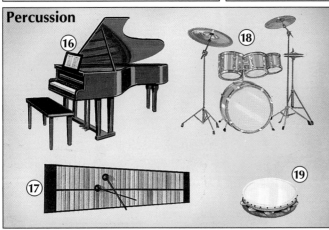

Other Instruments

3. flute
الفلوت

4. clarinet
الكلارينيت

5. oboe
مزمار

6. bassoon
زمخر

7. saxophone
ساكسفون

8. violin
كمان

9. cello
كمنجة كبيرة

10. bass
كمان ذو طبقة صوتية منخفضة

11. guitar
جيتار

12. trombone
المترددة (ترومبون)

13. trumpet / horn
البوق

14. tuba
التوبة

15. French horn
بوق فرنسي

16. piano
بيانو

17. xylophone
الخشبية

18. drums
طبول

19. tambourine
الرق

20. electric keyboard
لوحة مفاتيح كهربائية

21. accordion
أكورديون

22. organ
ارغن

STUDENT DRIVER

Profit Margin

It's a chair.

C'est une chaise.

1. art
فن

2. business education
تجارة وأعمال

3. chorus
الكورس

4. computer science
علم الكمبيوتر (الحاسوب)

5. driver's education
تعلم السواقة

6. economics
اقتصاد

7. English as a second language
اللغة الانجليزية كلغة ثانية

8. foreign language
لغة أجنبية

9. home economics
التدبير المنزلي

10. industrial arts / shop
ورشة الفنون الصناعية

11. PE (physical education)
رياضة

12. theater arts
مسرح

More vocabulary

core course: a subject students have to take

elective: a subject students choose to take

Share your answers.

1. What are your favorite subjects?

2. In your opinion, what subjects are most important? Why?

3. What foreign languages are taught in your school?

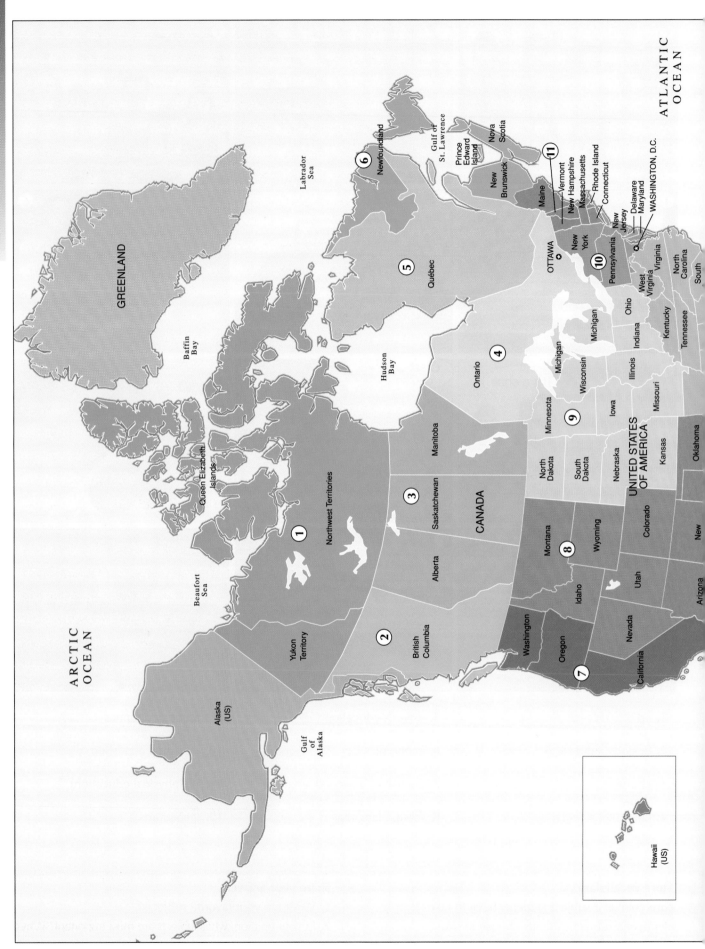

ATLANTIC OCEAN

ARCTIC OCEAN

GREENLAND

Baffin Bay

Labrador Sea

Beaufort Sea

Queen Elizabeth Islands

Northwest Territories

Hudson Bay

Gulf of St. Lawrence

Newfoundland

Québec

Ontario

Manitoba

Saskatchewan

Alberta

British Columbia

Yukon Territory

Alaska (US)

Gulf of Alaska

CANADA

OTTAWA

Prince Edward Island

Nova Scotia

New Brunswick

Maine

Vermont

New Hampshire

Massachusetts

Rhode Island

Connecticut

New York

Pennsylvania

New Jersey

Delaware

Maryland

WASHINGTON, D.C.

West Virginia

Virginia

North Carolina

South

Ohio

Indiana

Kentucky

Tennessee

Michigan

Michigan

Wisconsin

Illinois

Minnesota

Iowa

Missouri

North Dakota

South Dakota

Nebraska

Kansas

Oklahoma

UNITED STATES OF AMERICA

Montana

Wyoming

Colorado

New

Idaho

Utah

Arizona

Washington

Oregon

Nevada

California

Hawaii (US)

① ② ③ ④ ⑤ ⑥ ⑦ ⑧ ⑨ ⑩ ⑪

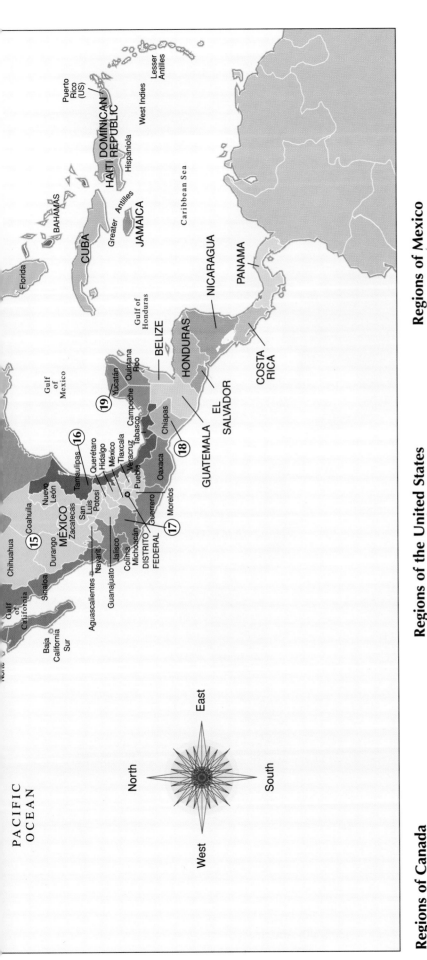

PACIFIC OCEAN

Florida
BAHAMAS
CUBA
Puerto Rico (US)
HAITI
DOMINICAN REPUBLIC
Hispaniola
JAMAICA
Greater Antilles
West Indies
Lesser Antilles
Caribbean Sea
NICARAGUA
PANAMA
COSTA RICA
EL SALVADOR
HONDURAS
Gulf of Honduras
BELIZE
GUATEMALA
Gulf of Mexico
Quintana Roo
Yucatán
Campeche
Tabasco
Chiapas
Veracruz
Oaxaca
Puebla
Morelos
Tlaxcala
México
Hidalgo
Querétaro
Guerrero
Michoacán
DISTRITO FEDERAL
Colima
Jalisco
Guanajuato
Nayarit
Aguascalientes
San Luis Potosí
Zacatecas
MÉXICO
Durango
Sinaloa
Nuevo León
Coahuila
Chihuahua
Tamaulipas
Gulf of California
Baja California Sur

⑮ ⑯ ⑰ ⑱ ⑲

Compass: North, East, South, West

Regions of Canada
أقاليم كندا

1. Northern Canada شمال كندا
2. British Columbia كولومبيا البريطانية
3. The Prairie Provinces مناطق المروج
4. Ontario أونتاريو
5. Québec كيبيك
6. The Atlantic Provinces مناطق الأطلنطي

Regions of the United States
أقاليم الولايات المتحدة

7. The Pacific States/the West Coast ولايات المهادي/الساحل الغربي
8. The Rocky Mountain States ولايات جبال الروكي
9. The Midwest الغرب الأوسط
10. The Mid-Atlantic States ولايات منطقة الأطلنطي الوسطى
11. New England نيو انجلاند
12. The Southwest الجنوب الغربي
13. The Southeast/the South الجنوب الشرقي/الجنوب

Regions of Mexico
أقاليم المكسيك

14. The Pacific Northwest الشمال الغربي المهادي
15. The Plateau of Mexico سهول المكسيك
16. The Gulf Coastal Plain سهول ساحل الخليج
17. The Southern Uplands المرتفعات الجنوبية
18. The Chiapas Highlands مرتفعات شياباس
19. The Yucatan Peninsula شبه جزيرة اليوكاتان

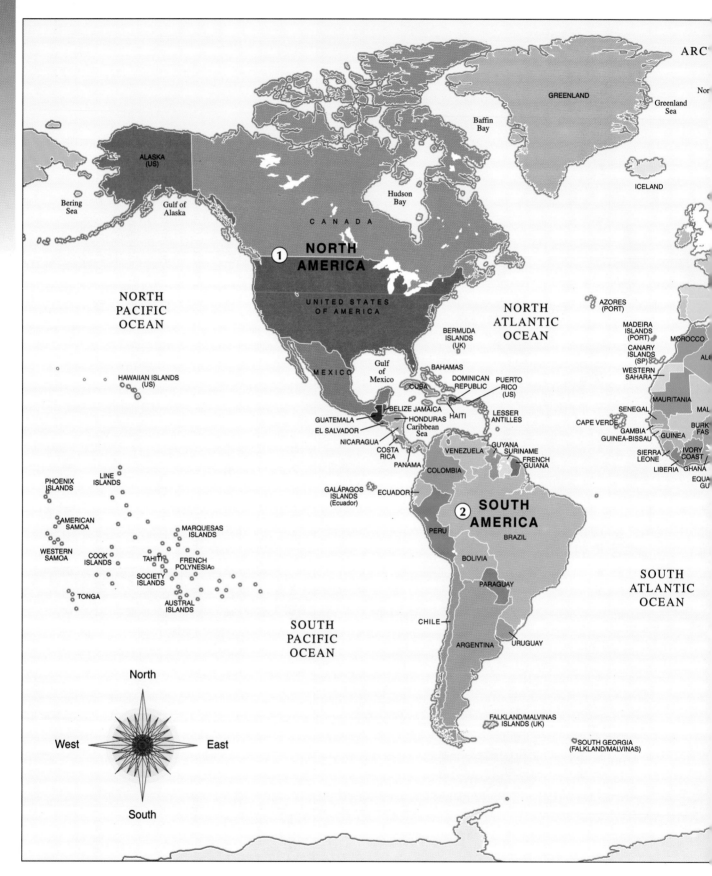

ARC

GREENLAND

Nor

Greenland
Sea

ALASKA
(US)

Baffin
Bay

ICELAND

Bering
Sea

Gulf of
Alaska

Hudson
Bay

CANADA

NORTH
PACIFIC
OCEAN

① NORTH
AMERICA

UNITED STATES
OF AMERICA

NORTH
ATLANTIC
OCEAN

AZORES
(PORT)

MEXICO

Gulf
of
Mexico

BERMUDA
ISLANDS
(UK)

BAHAMAS

MADEIRA
ISLANDS
(PORT)

MOROCCO

CANARY
ISLANDS
(SP)

CUBA

DOMINICAN
REPUBLIC

PUERTO
RICO
(US)

WESTERN
SAHARA

AL

HAWAIIAN ISLANDS
(US)

BELIZE JAMAICA

GUATEMALA
EL SALVADOR

HONDURAS
HAITI
Caribbean
Sea

LESSER
ANTILLES

MAURITANIA

SENEGAL

MAL

NICARAGUA

COSTA
RICA

PANAMA

CAPE VERDE

GAMBIA
GUINEA-BISSAU

GUINEA

BURK
FAS

VENEZUELA

GUYANA
SURINAME

FRENCH
GUIANA

SIERRA
LEONE

IVORY
COAST

LIBERIA

GHANA

EQUA
GU

PHOENIX
ISLANDS

LINE
ISLANDS

COLOMBIA

GALÁPAGOS
ISLANDS
(Ecuador)

ECUADOR

② SOUTH
AMERICA

AMERICAN
SAMOA

MARQUESAS
ISLANDS

PERU

BRAZIL

SOUTH
ATLANTIC
OCEAN

WESTERN
SAMOA

COOK
ISLANDS

TAHITI

FRENCH
POLYNESIA

BOLIVIA

SOCIETY
ISLANDS

TONGA

AUSTRAL
ISLANDS

PARAGUAY

SOUTH
PACIFIC
OCEAN

CHILE

North

West

East

ARGENTINA

URUGUAY

South

FALKLAND/MALVINAS
ISLANDS (UK)

SOUTH GEORGIA
(FALKLAND/MALVINAS)

Continents
القـــارات

1. North America
أمريكا الشمالية

2. South America
أمريكا الجنوبية

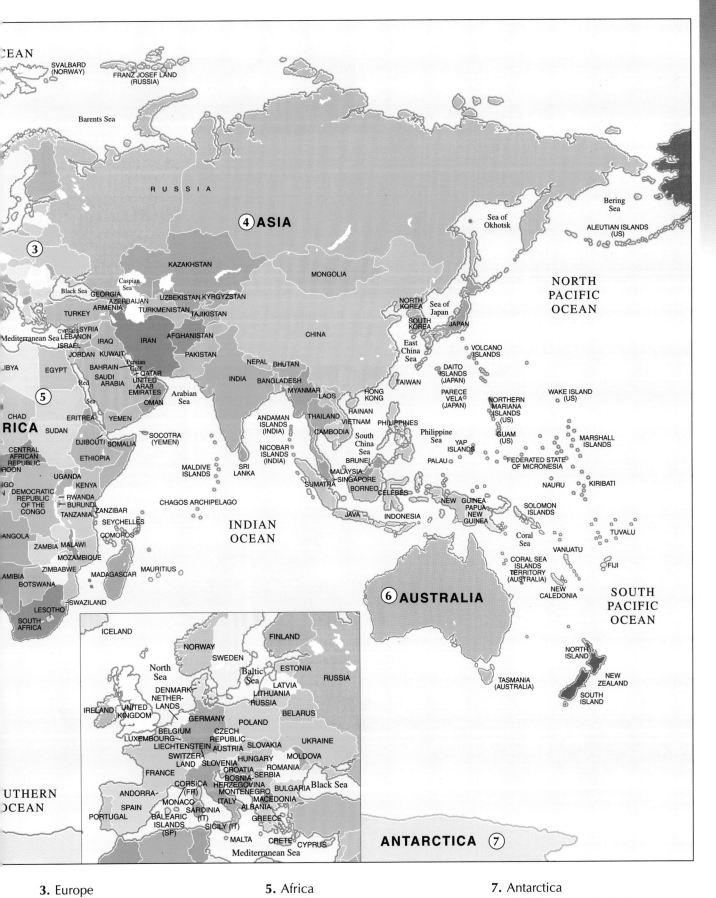

OCEAN

SVALBARD
(NORWAY)

FRANZ JOSEF LAND
(RUSSIA)

Barents Sea

RUSSIA

④ ASIA

③

Bering
Sea

Sea of
Okhotsk

ALEUTIAN ISLANDS
(US)

KAZAKHSTAN

MONGOLIA

NORTH
PACIFIC
OCEAN

Caspian
Sea

Black Sea

GEORGIA
AZERBAIJAN
ARMENIA
TURKEY
TURKMENISTAN

UZBEKISTAN KYRGYZSTAN

TAJIKISTAN

NORTH
KOREA
SOUTH
KOREA

Sea of
Japan

JAPAN

CYPRUS SYRIA
Mediterranean Sea LEBANON
ISRAEL
JORDAN KUWAIT
IRAQ
IRAN
AFGHANISTAN
CHINA

East
China
Sea

VOLCANO
ISLANDS

LIBYA
EGYPT
BAHRAIN
Persian
Gulf QATAR
SAUDI
ARABIA UNITED
ARAB
EMIRATES
OMAN
PAKISTAN
NEPAL
BHUTAN
INDIA
BANGLADESH
MYANMAR

TAIWAN

DAITO
ISLANDS
(JAPAN)

Red
Sea
Arabian
Sea
LAOS

HONG
KONG

PARECE
VELA
(JAPAN)

WAKE ISLAND
(US)

⑤

CHAD
SUDAN
ERITREA
YEMEN
SOCOTRA
(YEMEN)
ANDAMAN
ISLANDS
(INDIA)
THAILAND
VIETNAM
CAMBODIA
PHILIPPINES

NORTHERN
MARIANA
ISLANDS
(US)

AFRICA

HAINAN

Philippine
Sea

DJIBOUTI SOMALIA

CENTRAL
AFRICAN
REPUBLIC
ROON
ETHIOPIA
NICOBAR
ISLANDS
(INDIA)
South
China
Sea

GUAM
(US)

MARSHALL
ISLANDS

UGANDA
KENYA
MALDIVE
ISLANDS
SRI
LANKA
BRUNEI
MALAYSIA
YAP
ISLANDS

FEDERATED STATE
OF MICRONESIA

IGO
DEMOCRATIC
REPUBLIC
OF THE
CONGO
RWANDA
BURUNDI
TANZANIA
ZANZIBAR

SINGAPORE
SUMATRA
BORNEO
CELEBES
PALAU

NAURU
KIRIBATI

CHAGOS ARCHIPELAGO
JAVA
INDONESIA

NEW GUINEA
PAPUA
NEW
GUINEA

SOLOMON
ISLANDS

ANGOLA
SEYCHELLES
COMOROS
INDIAN
OCEAN

TUVALU

ZAMBIA MALAWI
MOZAMBIQUE

Coral
Sea

VANUATU

ZIMBABWE
MAURITIUS
AMIBIA
BOTSWANA
MADAGASCAR

CORAL SEA
ISLANDS
TERRITORY
(AUSTRALIA)
NEW
CALEDONIA

FIJI

SOUTH
PACIFIC
OCEAN

SWAZILAND
LESOTHO
SOUTH
AFRICA

⑥ AUSTRALIA

NORTH
ISLAND

ICELAND

FINLAND

NORWAY
SWEDEN

North
Sea
Baltic
Sea
ESTONIA
LATVIA
RUSSIA
TASMANIA
(AUSTRALIA)
NEW
ZEALAND
SOUTH
ISLAND

DENMARK
NETHER-
LANDS
LITHUANIA
RUSSIA

IRELAND UNITED
KINGDOM
GERMANY
BELARUS

BELGIUM
LUXEMBOURG
LIECHTENSTEIN
POLAND
CZECH
REPUBLIC
AUSTRIA
SLOVAKIA
UKRAINE

SWITZER-
LAND
SLOVENIA
HUNGARY
MOLDOVA

FRANCE
CROATIA
ROMANIA
BOSNIA
HERZEGOVINA
SERBIA

CORSICA
(FR)
MONTENEGRO
BULGARIA
Black Sea

ANDORRA
ITALY
MACEDONIA

MONACO
ALBANIA

SPAIN
SARDINIA
(T)
GREECE

PORTUGAL
BALEARIC
ISLANDS
(SP)
SICILY (IT)

MALTA
CRETE
CYPRUS

Mediterranean Sea

UTHERN
OCEAN

ANTARCTICA ⑦

125

Energy and the Environment الطاقـة والبيئـة

Energy resources موارد الطاقة

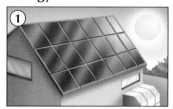

1. solar energy
الطاقة الشمسية

2. wind
ريح

3. natural gas
غاز طبيعي

4. coal
فحم

5. hydroelectric power
طاقة كهرمائية

6. oil/petroleum
النفط/ البترول

7. geothermal energy
طاقة حرارية أرضية

8. nuclear energy
طاقة نووية

Pollution تلوَّث

9. hazardous waste
نفايات خطرة

10. air pollution/smog
تلويث الجو

11. acid rain
مطر حمضي

12. water pollution
تلوّث المياه

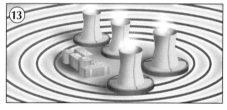

13. radiation
أشعة

14. pesticide poisoning
تسمم من مبيدات الحشرات

15. oil spill
انسكاب البترول

Conservation صيانة الموارد الطبيعية

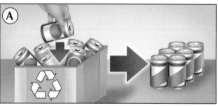

A. recycle
يعيد/ تعيد الاستعمال

B. save water/conserve water
يقتصد/ تقتصد بالماء

C. save energy/conserve energy
يقتصد/ تقتصد بالطاقة

Share your answers.

1. How do you heat your home?

2. Do you have a gas stove or an electric stove?

3. What are some ways you can save energy when it's cold?

4. Do you recycle? What products do you recycle?

5. Does your market have recycling bins?

126

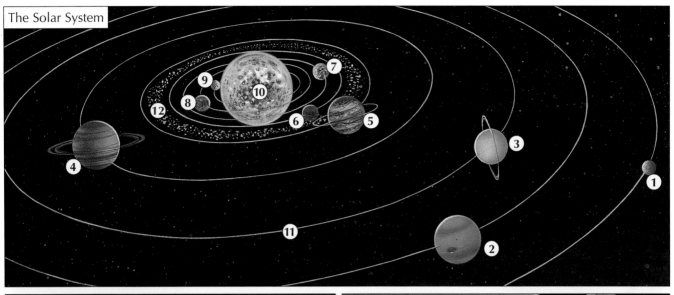

The Solar System

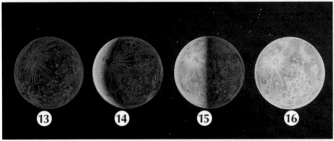

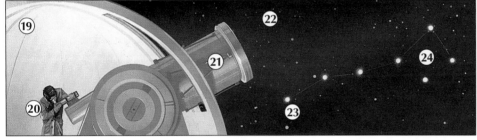

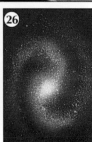

The planets
الكواكب السيارة

1. Pluto
   بلوتو
2. Neptune
   نبتون
3. Uranus
   أورانوس
4. Saturn
   زحل
5. Jupiter
   جوبتر
6. Mars
   المريخ (مارس)

7. Earth
   الأرض
8. Venus
   فينوس
9. Mercury
   عطارد

10. sun
    الشمس
11. orbit
    مدار
12. asteroid belt
    حزام الكواكب
    الصغيرة (كويكب)

13. new moon
    هلال
14. crescent moon
    هلال
15. quarter moon
    ربع قمر
16. full moon
    بدر
17. astronaut
    رجل فضاء
18. space station
    محطة فضاء
19. observatory
    مرصد

20. astronomer
    عالم فلكي
21. telescope
    تلسكوب
22. space
    فضاء
23. star
    نجم
24. constellation
    مجموعة نجوم متألقة
25. comet
    مذنِب
26. galaxy
    المجرّة

More vocabulary

lunar eclipse: when the earth is between the sun and the moon

solar eclipse: when the moon is between the earth and the sun

Share your answers.

1. Do you know the names of any constellations?
2. How do you feel when you look up at the night sky?
3. Is the night sky in the U.S. the same as in your country?

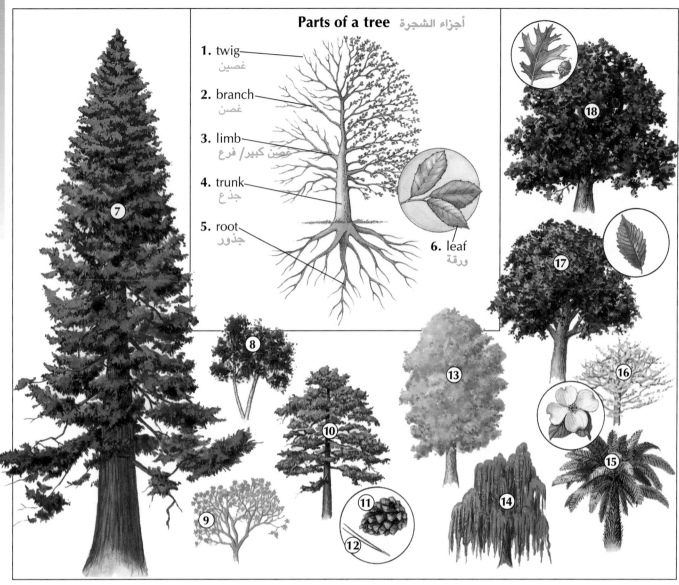

Parts of a tree   أجزاء الشجرة

1. twig
غصين

2. branch
غصن

3. limb
غصين كبير/ فرع

4. trunk
جذع

5. root
جذور

6. leaf
ورقة

7. redwood
خشب أحمر

8. birch
بتولا (شجر القضبان)

9. magnolia
مغنولية

10. pine
شجر الصنوبر

11. pinecone
كوز صنوبر

12. needle
ورقة إبرية

13. maple
قيقب

14. willow
صفصاف

15. palm
نخل

16. dogwood
قرانيا

17. elm
دردار

18. oak
سنديان

Plants   نباتات

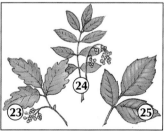

19. holly
البهشية

20. berries
توت

21. cactus
صبار

22. vine
كرمة

23. poison oak
بلوط سام

24. poison sumac
سماق سام

25. poison ivy
لبلاب سام

Parts of a flower أجزاء زهرة

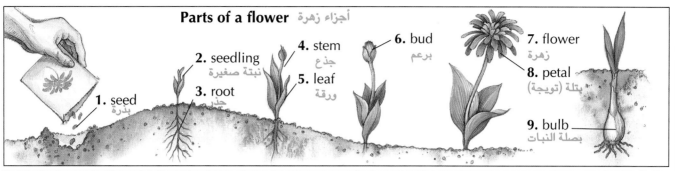

1. seed
بذرة

2. seedling
نبتة صغيرة

3. root
جذر

4. stem
جذع

5. leaf
ورقة

6. bud
برعم

7. flower
زهرة

8. petal
بتلة (تويجة)

9. bulb
بصلة النبات

10. sunflower عباد الشمس	**15.** rose وردة	**20.** iris سوسن	**25.** crocus زعفران
11. tulip زنبقة	**16.** gardenia الغردينيا	**21.** jasmine ياسمين	**26.** daffodil النرجس البري
12. hibiscus خبيزة	**17.** orchid السحلبية	**22.** violet ليلك	**27.** bouquet باقة أزهار
13. marigold قطيفة	**18.** carnation الفل	**23.** poinsettia البونسيتة	**28.** thorn شوكة
14. daisy زهرة الربيع	**19.** chrysanthemum أقحوان	**24.** lily الزنبق	**29.** houseplant نبتة منزلية

Parts of a fish أجزاء السمكة

Sea animals حيوانات البحر

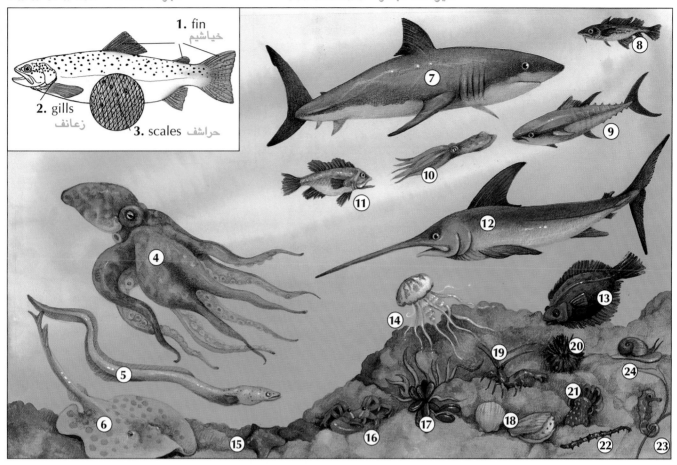

1. fin خياشيم
2. gills زعانف
3. scales حراشف

4. octopus أخطبوط	**11.** bass القاروس	**18.** scallop الأسقوب
5. eel الأنقليس	**12.** swordfish أبو سيف	**19.** shrimp قريدس
6. ray شفنين بحري	**13.** flounder السمك المفلطح	**20.** sea urchin قنفذ البحر
7. shark القرش	**14.** jellyfish السمك الهلامي (قنديل البحر)	**21.** sea anemone شقيق البحر
8. cod القد	**15.** starfish نجم البحر	**22.** worm دودة
9. tuna التونة (سمك التن)	**16.** crab سلطعون	**23.** sea horse فرس البحر
10. squid الحبار	**17.** mussel بلح البحر	**24.** snail بزاقة

Amphibians البرمائيات

25. frog ضفدع	**26.** newt سمندل الماء	**27.** salamander السمندر	**28.** toad العلجوم

130

Sea mammals الثدييات البحرية

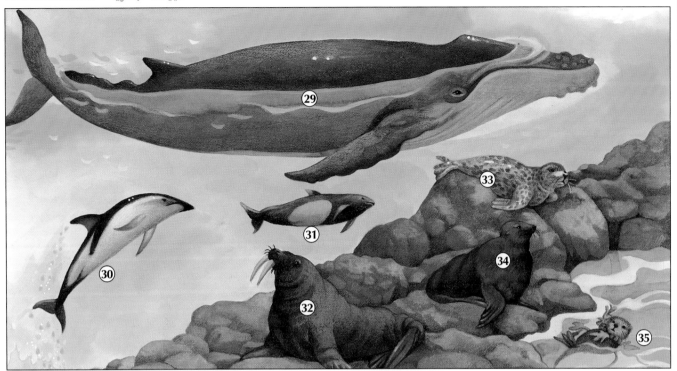

29. whale
حوت

30. dolphin
دلفين

31. porpoise
خنزير البحر

32. walrus
الفظ

33. seal
الفقمة

34. sea lion
أسد البحر

35. otter
القضاعة

Reptiles الزواحف

36. alligator
تمساح

37. crocodile
القاطور (تمساح اميركا)

38. rattlesnake
المجلجلة/ ذات الأجراس

39. garter snake
الغرطر

40. cobra
الصل (كوبرا)

41. lizard
السحلية

42. turtle
سلحفاة

Birds, Insects, and Arachnids الطيور والحشرات، والعنكبوتيات

Parts of a bird أجزاء الطير

1. beak / bill
منقار

2. wing
جناح

3. nest
عش

4. claw
مخلب

5. feather
ريشة

6. owl بوم	**9.** woodpecker نقار الخشب	**12.** penguin البطريق	**15.** peacock طاووس
7. blue jay القيق الأزرق/ الزرياب	**10.** eagle صقر	**13.** duck بط	**16.** pigeon حمامة
8. sparrow عصفور دوري	**11.** hummingbird الطنان	**14.** goose وزة (أوزة)	**17.** robin أبو الحناء

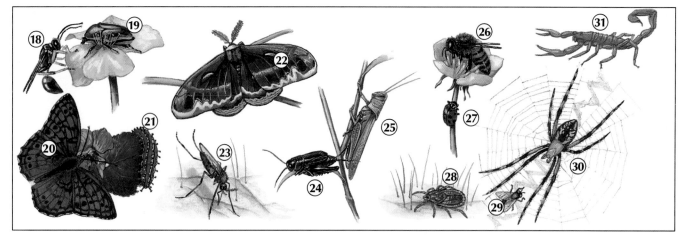

18. wasp زنبور	**22.** moth عثة	**26.** honeybee نحلة عسل	**30.** spider عنكبوت
19. beetle خنفساء	**23.** mosquito بعوضة	**27.** ladybug الدعسوقة	**31.** scorpion عقرب
20. butterfly فراشة	**24.** cricket صرار الليل	**28.** tick القرادة	
21. caterpillar يرقانة	**25.** grasshopper الجندب	**29.** fly ذبابة	

132

Farm animals حيوانات المزارع

1. goat
ماعز

2. donkey
حمار

3. cow
بقرة

4. horse
حصان

5. hen
دجاجة

6. rooster
ديك

7. sheep
خروف

8. pig
خنزير

Pets الحيوانات المنزلية

9. cat
هرة

10. kitten
هرة صغيرة

11. dog
كلب

12. puppy
جرو

13. rabbit
أرنب

14. guinea pig
خنزير هندي

15. parakeet
ببغاء صغير

16. goldfish
سمك ذهبي

Rodents القوارض

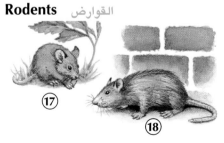

17. mouse
فأر

18. rat
جرذ

19. gopher
الغوفر (سنجاب أمريكي)

20. chipmunk
الصيدناني (سنجاب أمريكي صغير مخطط)

21. squirrel
سنجاب

22. prairie dog
كلب المروج

More vocabulary

Wild animals live, eat, and raise their young away from people, in the forests, mountains, plains, etc.

Domesticated animals work for people or live with them.

Share your answers.

1. Do you have any pets? any farm animals?

2. Which of these animals are in your neighborhood? Which are not?

1. moose
الموظ

2. mountain lion
أسد الجبال (الكوجر)

3. coyote
القيوط (ذئب أمريكي)

4. opossum
الأبوسوم

5. wolf
ذئب

6. buffalo / bison
جاموس

7. bat
خفاش

8. armadillo
المدرع

9. beaver
قندس

10. porcupine
الشيهم / النيص

11. bear
دب

12. skunk
الظربان

13. raccoon
الراكون

14. deer
غزال

15. fox
ثعلب

16. antler
قرن الوعل

17. hoof
حافر

18. whiskers
السبلات

19. coat / fur
فروة

20. paw
كف الحيوان ذات البراثن

21. horn
قرن

22. tail
ذنب

23. quill
أشواك القنفذ

24. anteater آكل النمل	**30.** gorilla الغوريلا	**36.** lion أسد	**42.** elephant فيل
25. leopard النمر	**31.** hyena الضبع	**37.** tiger نمر	**43.** hippopotamus فرس النهر
26. llama اللامة	**32.** baboon سعدان أفريقي	**38.** camel جمل	**44.** kangaroo الكنغر
27. monkey السعدان	**33.** giraffe زرافة	**39.** panther النمر الأمريكي	**45.** koala الكوال
28. chimpanzee الشمبانزي	**34.** zebra الحمار الوحشي	**40.** orangutan إنسان الغاب	**46.** platypus البلاتبوس
29. rhinoceros الكركدن	**35.** antelope الظبي	**41.** panda البندة	

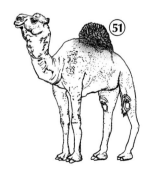

47. trunk خرطوم	**48.** tusk ناب	**49.** mane العرف	**50.** pouch جيب	**51.** hump حدبة

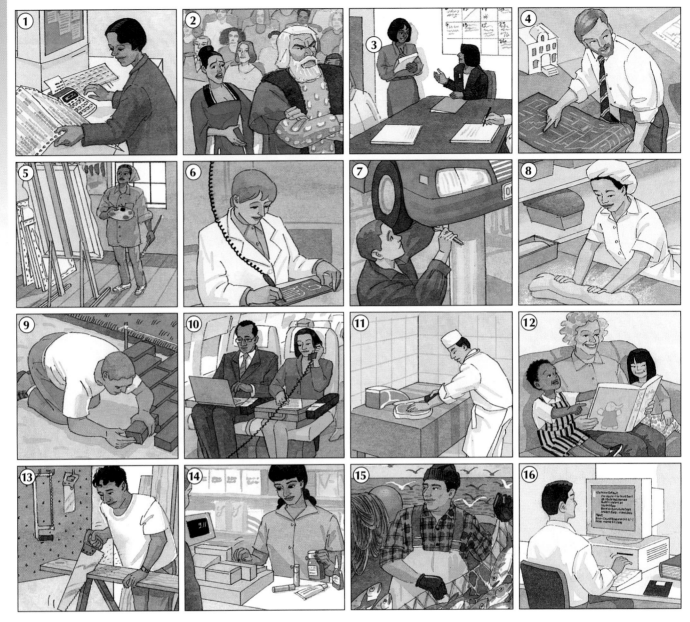

1. accountant محاسبة	**7.** auto mechanic ميكانيكي سيارات	**13.** carpenter نجار
2. actor ممثل	**8.** baker فران/ خبّازة	**14.** cashier أمينة صندوق
3. administrative assistant سكرتيرة ادارية	**9.** bricklayer بناء بالآجر	**15.** commercial fisher صياد تجاري
4. architect مهندس معماري	**10.** businessman/businesswoman رجل أعمال/ امرأة أعمال	**16.** computer programmer مبرمج كمبيوتر (حاسوب)
5. artist فنانة	**11.** butcher لحام/ جزار	
6. assembler عاملة تجميع أو تركيب	**12.** caregiver/baby-sitter حاضن/ حاضنة أطفال	

Use the new language.

1. Who works outside?

2. Who works inside?

3. Who makes things?

4. Who uses a computer?

5. Who wears a uniform?

6. Who sells things?

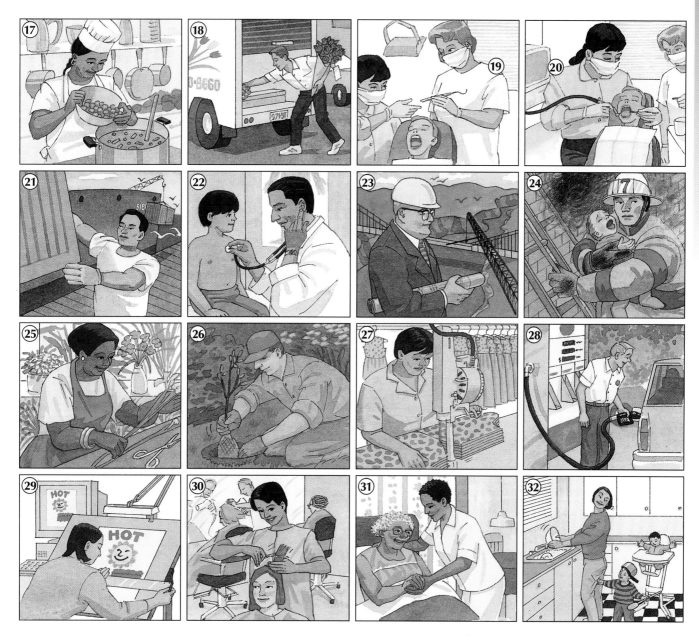

17. cook
طباخة

18. delivery person
موزع

19. dental assistant
مساعد/ ـة طبيب أسنان

20. dentist
طبيب/ ـة أسنان

21. dockworker
عامل مراكب

22. doctor
طبيب

23. engineer
مهندس

24. firefighter
اطفائي

25. florist
بائعة زهور

26. gardener
بستاني

27. garment worker
خيّاطة

28. gas station attendant
عامل في محطة بنزين

29. graphic artist
اخصائي فنون تخطيطية

30. hairdresser
مزينة شعر

31. home attendant
مساعدة منزلية

32. homemaker
ربة بيت

Share your answers.

1. Do you know people who have some of these jobs? What do they say about their work?

2. Which of these jobs are available in your city?

3. For which of these jobs do you need special training?

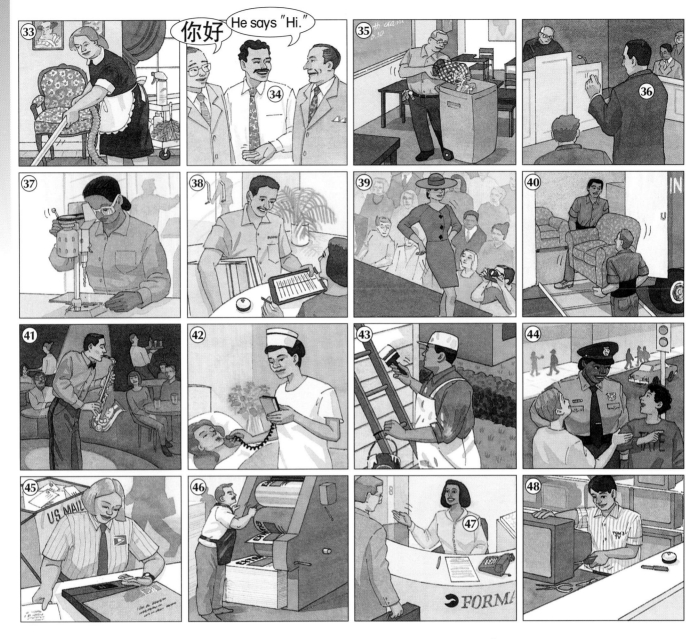

33. housekeeper
    مدبرة منزل
34. interpreter/translator
    مترجم شفهي/ تحريري
35. janitor/custodian
    حاجب/ بواب
36. lawyer
    محامي
37. machine operator
    عامل ميكانيكي
38. messenger/courier
    ساعي/ رسول

39. model
    عارضة أزياء
40. mover
    عامل نقليات
41. musician
    موسيقي
42. nurse
    ممرضة
43. painter
    دهّان
44. police officer
    شرطي

45. postal worker
    موظف بريد
46. printer
    عامل طباعة
47. receptionist
    موظفة استقبال
48. repair person
    اخصائي تصليح

Talk about each of the jobs or occupations.

She's a housekeeper. She works in a hotel.

He's an interpreter. He works for the government.

She's a nurse. She works with patients.

49. reporter
مراسل صحفي

50. salesclerk / salesperson
موظف مبيعات

51. sanitation worker
عامل نظافة

52. secretary
سكرتيرة

53. server
نادل

54. serviceman / servicewoman
جندي / جندية

55. stock clerk
موظف بورصة

56. store owner
صاحب محل

57. student
طالب

58. teacher / instructor
معلم / مدرس

59. telemarketer
مسوَّق / ـة هاتفيا

60. travel agent
وكيل سفريات

61. truck driver
سائق شاحنة

62. veterinarian
طبيب بيطري

63. welder
لحام

64. writer / author
كاتب / مؤلف

Talk about your job or the job you want.

What do you do?

   I'm a salesclerk. I work in a store.

What do you want to do?

   I want to be a veterinarian. I want to work with animals.

A. **assemble** components
يجمَع/ تجمَع القطع

B. **assist** medical patients
يساعد المرضى

C. **cook**
يطبخ

D. **do** manual labor
يقوم بأعمال يدوية

E. **drive** a truck
يسوق شاحنة

F. **operate** heavy machinery
يشغل آلات ثقيلة

G. **repair** appliances
يصلح الأدوات

H. **sell** cars
يبيع سيارات

I. **sew** clothes
يخيّط/ تخيّط ثياب

J. **speak** another language
يتكلم لغة ثانية

K. **supervise** people
تشرف على الموظفين

L. **take care** of children
تعتني بالأطفال

M. **type**
يطبع/ تطبع

N. **use** a cash register
يستعمل مسجلة النقود

O. **wait on** customers
تقوم على خدمة الزبائن

P. **work** on a computer
يستعمل الكمبيوتر

More vocabulary

act: to perform in a play, movie, or TV show

fly: to pilot an airplane

teach: to instruct, to show how to do something

Share your answers.

1. What job skills do you have? Where did you learn them?

2. What job skills do you want to learn?

A. talk to friends
يبحث الأمر مع صديق

B. look at a job board
يراجع لوح الأعمال الشاغرة

C. look for a help wanted sign
يبحث عن لافتات الأعمال الشاغرة

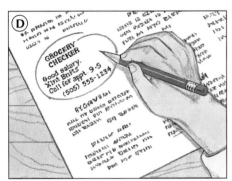

D. look in the classifieds
يراجع الاعلانات المبَوبة في الصحف

E. call for information
يتصل للحصول على معلومات

F. ask about the hours
يسأل عن ساعات العمل

G. fill out an application
يملأ طلب تقدم للعمل

H. go on an interview
يذهب للمقابلة

I. talk about your experience
يتكلم عن خبراته

J. ask about benefits
يسأل عن المنافع كالتأمين والاجازة

K. inquire about the salary
يستفسر عن الراتب

L. get hired
يحصل على الوظيفة

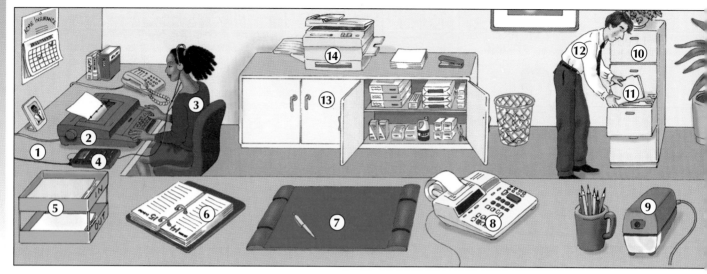

1. desk
   مكتب

2. typewriter
   آلة كاتبة

3. secretary
   سكرتيرة

4. microcassette transcriber
   آلة نقل المعلومات من كاسيت

5. stacking tray
   حوامل مركبة

6. desk calendar
   روزنامة/ تقويم مكتب

7. desk pad
   غطاء مكتب

8. calculator
   آلة حاسبة

9. electric pencil sharpener
   مبراة أقلام كهربائية

10. file cabinet
    خزانة ملفات

11. file folder
    حافظة ملفات/ دوسية

12. file clerk
    موظف تنظيم الملفات

13. supply cabinet
    خزانة المؤن

14. photocopier
    ماكينة تصوير مستندات

A. **take** a message
   تسجل بلاغ

B. **fax** a letter
   ترسل رسالة بالفاكس

C. **transcribe** notes
   تدوّن ملاحظات

D. **type** a letter
   تطبع رسالة

E. **make** copies
   تعمل نسخ

F. **collate** papers
   ترتب الأوراق

G. **staple**
   تخرز/ تكبّس الأوراق

H. **file** papers
   تحفظ الأوراق في ملفات

Practice taking messages.

Hello. My name is Sara Scott. Is Mr. Lee in?

Not yet. Would you like to leave a message?

Yes. Please ask him to call me at 555-4859.

Share your answers.

1. Which office equipment do you know how to use?
2. Which jobs does a file clerk do?
3. Which jobs does a secretary do?

142

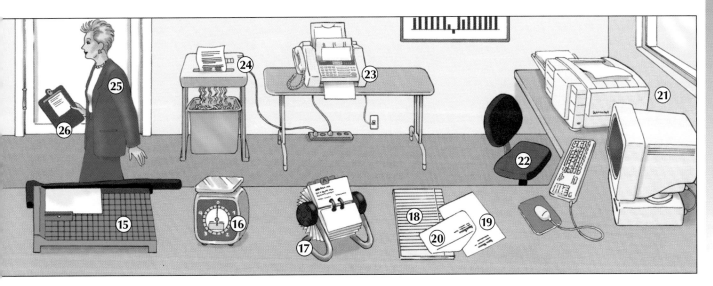

15. paper cutter
قاطعة أوراق

16. postal scale
ميزان بريدي

17. rotary card file
ملف بطاقات دوّار

18. legal pad
كراسة ورق طويل

19. letterhead paper
ورقة طبع في رأسها اسم المؤسسة

20. envelope
مغلف

21. computer workstation
جهاز كمبيوتر

22. swivel chair
كرسي دوّار

23. fax machine
جهاز الفاكسيميليا

24. paper shredder
آلة تمزيق الورق

25. office manager
مدير مكتب

26. clipboard
اللوح المشبكي

27. appointment book
دفتر مواعيد

28. stapler
خرّازة/ كبّاسة

29. staple
خرزة/ دبوس

30. organizer
دفتر منظّم

31. typewriter cartridge
خرطوشة آلة كاتبة

32. mailer
مغلف بريد

33. correction fluid
سائل تصحيح

34. Post-it notes
مذكرات قابلة للتعليق

35. label
بطاقات تعريف

36. notepad
دفتر ملاحظات

37. glue
صمغ

38. rubber cement
اللصاق المطاطي

39. clear tape
شريط لاصق بدون لون

40. rubber stamp
ختم مطاطي

41. ink pad
لبادة تحبير/ مختمة

42. packing tape
شريط حزم لاصق

43. pushpin
دبوس كبسي

44. paper clip
مشبك ورق

45. rubber band
شريط (طوق) مطاطي

Use the new language.

1. Which items keep things together?

2. Which items are used to mail packages?

3. Which items are made of paper?

Share your answers.

1. Which office supplies do students use?

2. Where can you buy them?

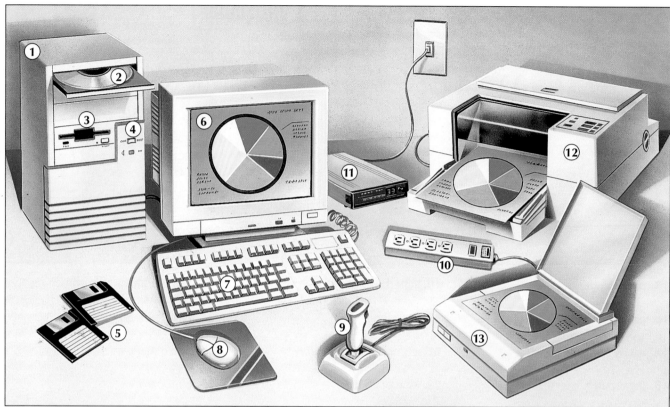

Hardware
الأجهزة

1. CPU (central processing unit)
وحدة المعالجة المركزية

2. CD-ROM disc
قرص سي دي روم

3. disk drive
جهاز ادارة القرص

4. power switch
مفتاح الطاقة

5. disk/floppy
قرص

6. monitor/screen
شاشة

7. keyboard
لوحة مفاتيح

8. mouse
ماوس

9. joystick
عصا توجيه

10. surge protector
جهاز ضد اشتداد التيار

11. modem
مودم

12. printer
طابعة

13. scanner
ماسحة تصوير

14. laptop
كمبيوتر نقال

15. trackball
كرة توجيه المنزلقة

16. cable
كبل

17. port
منفذ

18. motherboard
لوح الأم الرئيسية

19. slot
فتحة

20. hard disk drive
قرص صلب

Software
البرامج

21. program/application
برنامج

22. user's manual
كتيب المستخدم

More vocabulary

data: information that a computer can read

memory: how much data a computer can hold

speed: how fast a computer can work with data

Share your answers.

1. Can you use a computer?

2. How did you learn? in school? from a book? by yourself?

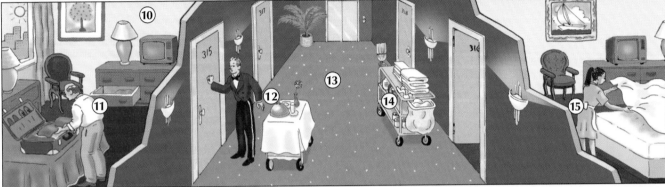

1. valet parking
مستخدم خصوصي لايقاف السيارات

2. doorman
بوّاب

3. lobby
صالة الاستقبال

4. bell captain
رئيس مستخدمي نقل الأمتعة

5. bellhop
خادم فندق

6. luggage cart
عربة لنقل الأمتعة

7. gift shop
محل بيع الهدايا

8. front desk
مكتب التسجيل

9. desk clerk
موظف فندق

10. guest room
غرفة ضيوف

11. guest
نزيل

12. room service
خدمات الطعام في الغرفة

13. hall
قاعة

14. housekeeping cart
عربة تجهيز الغرف

15. housekeeper
عاملة تجهيز الغرف

16. pool
بركة سباحة

17. pool service
خدمات بركة السباحة

18. ice machine
ماكينة الثلج

19. meeting room
غرفة اجتماعات

20. ballroom
قاعة الرقص

More vocabulary

concierge: the hotel worker who helps guests find restaurants and interesting places to go

service elevator: an elevator for hotel workers

Share your answers.

1. Does this look like a hotel in your city? Which one?

2. Which hotel job is the most difficult?

3. How much does it cost to stay in a hotel in your city?

1. front office
المكتب الأمامي

2. factory owner
صاحب المصنع

3. designer
مصمِّم

4. time clock
ساعة توقيت

5. line supervisor
المشرف على خط التجميع

6. factory worker
عامل

7. parts
قطع

8. assembly line
خط تجميع

9. warehouse
مستودع

10. order puller
مسؤول احضار الطلبات

11. hand truck
عربة نقل يدوية

12. conveyor belt
سير ناقل

13. packer
عامل تعبئة

14. forklift
مرفاع شوكي

15. shipping clerk
عامل شحن

16. loading dock
منصة تحميل

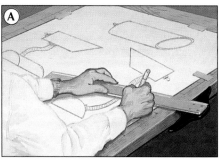

A. design
يصمِّم

B. manufacture
يصنع

C. ship
يشحن

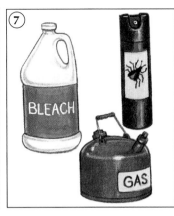
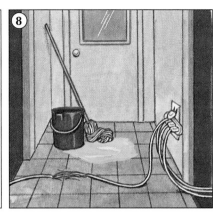

1. electrical hazard
مخاطر كهربائية

2. flammable
قابل للاشتعال

3. poison
سام

4. corrosive
تأكسد

5. biohazard
خطر بيولوجي

6. radioactive
مواد مشعّة

7. hazardous materials
مواد خطرة

8. dangerous situation
وضع خطر

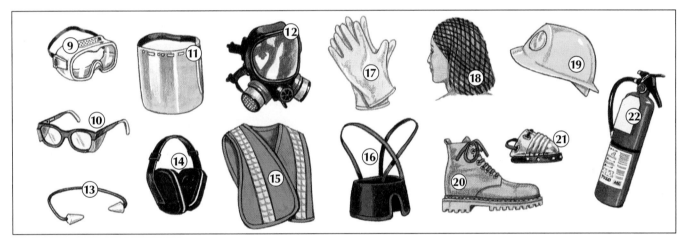

9. safety goggles
منظار وقاية

10. safety glasses
نظارات سلامة

11. safety visor
قناع وقاية

12. respirator
كمامة ضد الغازات السامة

13. earplugs
سدادة أذن

14. safety earmuffs
واقية الآذان

15. safety vest
سترة الوقاية

16. back support
حزام لدعم الظهر

17. latex gloves
قفازات مطاطية

18. hair net
شبكة تغطية الشعر

19. hard hat
قبعة صلبة

20. safety boot
حذاء وقاية

21. toe guard
حامية أصابع القدم

22. fire extinguisher
مطفئة الحريق

23. careless
غير محترس

24. careful
محترس

Crops المحاصيل الزراعية

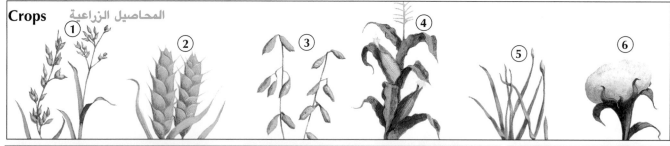

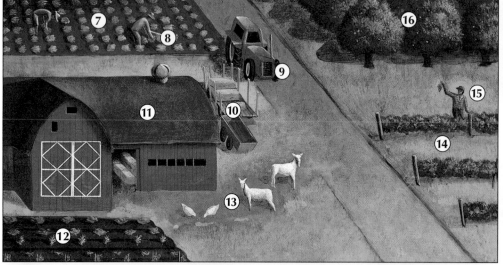

1. rice
الأرز

2. wheat
القمح

3. soybeans
الصويا

4. corn
الذرة

5. alfalfa
الفصفصة

6. cotton
القطن

7. field
حقل

8. farmworker
عامل مزرعة

9. tractor
تراكتور (جرارة)

10. farm equipment
معدات مزرعة

11. barn
حظيرة

12. vegetable garden
حديقة خضار

13. livestock
مواشي

14. vineyard
كرمة

15. farmer / grower
مزارع

16. orchard
بستان فاكهة

17. corral
زريبة

18. hay
قش

19. fence
سياج

20. hired hand
مستخدم مساعد

21. steers / cattle
ماشية

22. rancher
مربي مواشي

A. plant
يزرع

B. harvest
يحصد

C. milk
يحلب

D. feed
يقدم العلف

1. construction worker
عامل بناء

2. ladder
سلم

3. I beam/girder
عارضة

4. scaffolding
سقالة

5. cherry picker
رافعة ذات ذراع طويل

6. bulldozer
جرافة لشق الطرق

7. crane
مرفاع (ونش)

8. backhoe
مجرفة خلفية

9. jackhammer/pneumatic drill
ثقابة آلية

10. concrete
اسمنت

11. bricks
قرميد

12. trowel
المالج

13. insulation
مواد عازلة

14. stucco
جص

15. window pane
لوح زجاجي في نافذة

16. plywood
خشب رقائقي

17. wood/lumber
خشب

18. drywall
جدار داخلي

19. shingles
ألواح خشبية

20. pickax
معول

21. shovel
جاروف

22. sledgehammer
مطرقة ثقيلة/ المرزبة

A. **paint**
يطلي/ يدهن

B. **lay** bricks
يرصف القرميد

C. **measure**
يقيس

D. **hammer**
يدق

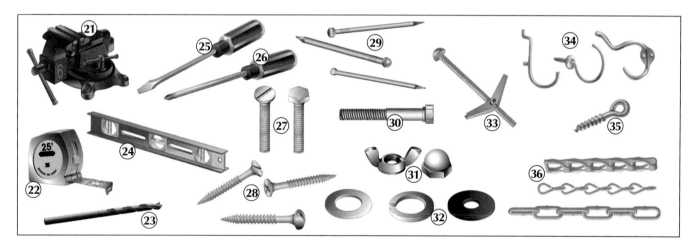

1. hammer
مطرقة

2. mallet
مطرقة خشبية

3. ax
فأس

4. handsaw
منشار يدوي

5. hacksaw
منشار معادن

6. C- clamp
قامطة تثبيت

7. pliers
زردية

8. electric drill
مثقاب كهربائي

9. power sander
ماكنة سنفرة للتنعيم

10. circular saw
منشار دائري

11. blade
نصلة / شفرة

12. router
مسحاج تخديد

21. vise
منجلة / ملزمة

22. tape measure
شريط قياس

23. drill bit
لقمة ثقب

24. level
الشاقول، ميزان البنائين

25. screwdriver
مفك براغي

26. Phillips screwdriver
مفك براغي مصلب الرأس

27. machine screw
برغي ربط ملولب

28. wood screw
برغي خشب

29. nail
مسمار

30. bolt
مسمار ملولب

31. nut
عزقة

32. washer
فلكة

33. toggle bolt
مسمار العقدة

34. hook
خطّاف / كلاب

35. eye hook
خطاف عروة

36. chain
سلسلة

Use the new language.

1. Which tools are used for plumbing?

2. Which tools are used for painting?

3. Which tools are used for electrical work?

4. Which tools are used for working with wood?

13. wire
سلك

14. extension cord
سلك تمديد

15. yardstick
عصا الياردة

16. pipe
أنبوب

17. fittings
تجهيزات

18. wood
خشب

19. spray gun
مرشة

20. paint
طلاء

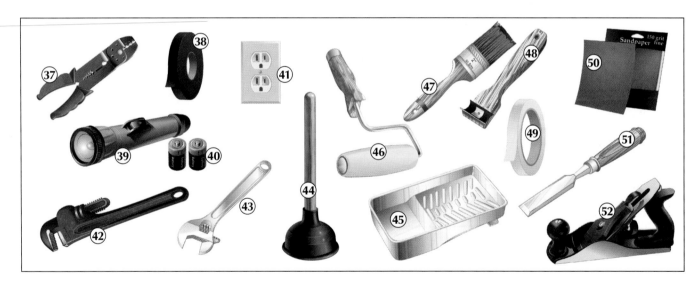

37. wire stripper
مقشّرة أسلاك

38. electrical tape
شريط لاصق للأسلاك الكهربائية

39. flashlight
مصباح جيب كهربائي

40. battery
بطارية

41. outlet
مأخذ التيار الكهربائي

42. pipe wrench
مفتاح أنابيب

43. wrench
مفتاح ربط

44. plunger
مضخة

45. paint pan
صينية طلاء

46. paint roller
فرشاة طلاء اسطوانية

47. paintbrush
فرشاة طلاء

48. scraper
مكشطة

49. masking tape
شريط لاصق للتغطية

50. sandpaper
ورق الزجاج

51. chisel
إزميل

52. plane
مسحاج/ فأرة النجار

Use the new language.

Look at **Household Problems and Repairs,**
pages **48–49.**

Name the tools you use to fix the problems you see.

Share your answers.

1. Which tools do you have in your home?

2. Which tools can be dangerous to use?

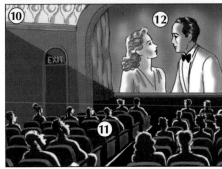

1. zoo
حديقة الحيوانات

2. animals
حيوانات

3. zookeeper
مسؤول حديقة الحيوانات

4. botanical gardens
حدائق طبيعية

5. greenhouse
الدفيئة/ مستنبت زجاجي

6. gardener
بستاني

7. art museum
متحف للفنون

8. painting
لوحات

9. sculpture
تماثيل

10. the movies
السينما

11. seat
مقعد

12. screen
شاشة

13. amusement park
مدينة ملاهي

14. puppet show
مسرح الدمي

15. roller coaster
الأفعوانية/ سكة مرتفعة

16. carnival
مهرجان/ كرنفال

17. rides
شوط

18. game
لعبة

19. county fair
معرض الملاهي

20. first place/first prize
المرتبة الأولى/ الجائزة الأولى

21. exhibition
معرض

22. swap meet/flea market
سوق المقايضة أو الخردوات

23. booth
كشك

24. merchandise
سلع

25. baseball game
لعبة بيسبول

26. stadium
مدرج/ استاد

27. announcer
مذيع

Talk about the places you like to go.

I like <u>animals</u>, so I go to <u>the zoo</u>.

I like <u>rides</u>, so I go to <u>carnivals</u>.

Share your answers.

1. Which of these places is interesting to you?

2. Which rides do you like at an amusement park?

3. What are some famous places to go to in your country?

1. **ball field**
   ملعب كرة

2. **bike path**
   ممر دراجات

3. **cyclist**
   راكب دراجة

4. **bicycle/bike**
   دراجة

5. **jump rope**
   حبل الوثب

6. **duck pond**
   بركة بط

7. **tennis court**
   ملعب كرة المضرب

8. **picnic table**
   طاولة نزهة

9. **tricycle**
   دراجة ثلاثية العجلات

10. **bench**
    البنك/ مقعد طويل

11. **water fountain**
    نافورة مياه للشرب

12. **swings**
    مراجيح

13. **slide**
    زلاقة

14. **climbing apparatus**
    قضبان تسلق

15. **sandbox**
    صندوق رمل

16. **seesaw**
    نواسة تأرجح

A. **pull** the wagon
   تسحب العربة

B. **push** the swing
   تدفع الأرجوحة

C. **climb** on the bars
   يتسلق/ تتسلق على القضبان

D. **picnic/have** a picnic
   يقوم/ تقوم بنزهة

1. camping
تخييم

2. boating
ركوب الزوارق

3. canoeing
ركوب الكنو (زوارق طويلة)

4. rafting
رياضة الطوف

5. fishing
الصيد

6. hiking
التنزه سيرا على الأقدام

7. backpacking
حمل الأمتعة على الظهر

8. mountain biking
ركوب الدراجات على الجبال

9. horseback riding
ركوب الخيل

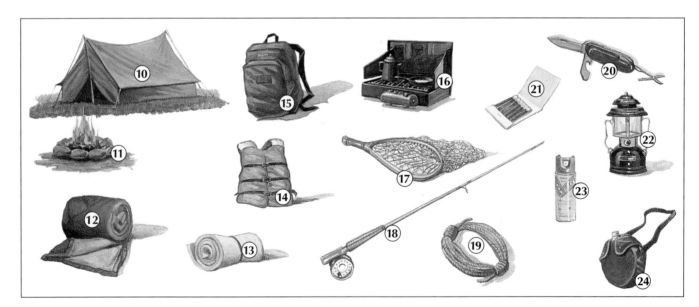

10. tent
خيمة

11. campfire
نار تخييم

12. sleeping bag
كيس نوم

13. foam pad
فرشة من الأسفنج

14. life vest
صدرية النجاة

15. backpack
حقيبة تحمل على الظهر

16. camping stove
موقد تخييم

17. fishing net
شبكة صيد

18. fishing pole
صنارة سمك

19. rope
حبل

20. multi-use knife
سكين متعدد الاستعمالات

21. matches
أعواد ثقاب/ كبريت

22. lantern
فانوس

23. insect repellent
مادة طاردة للحشرات

24. canteen
مزادة (قربة الماء)

1. ocean/water المحيط/ الماء	**10.** sand castle قلعة من الرمل	**19.** lifesaving device أداة انقاذ
2. fins زعانف	**11.** cooler صندوق تبريد	**20.** lifeguard station مركز للمنقذين
3. diving mask قناع غوص	**12.** shade ظل	**21.** seashell صدفة بحرية
4. sailboat زورق شراعي	**13.** sunscreen/sunblock مرهم واقي من أشعة الشمس	**22.** pail/bucket دلو
5. surfboard لوح ركوب الأمواج	**14.** beach chair كرسي للشاطئ	**23.** sand رمل
6. wave موجة	**15.** beach towel منشفة كبيرة للشاطئ	**24.** rock صخرة
7. wet suit بذلة غوص	**16.** pier رصيف ممتد في البحر	
8. scuba tank خزان اكسجين للغوص	**17.** sunbather شخص يأخذ حمام شمس	
9. beach umbrella مظلة للشاطئ	**18.** lifeguard منقذ	

More vocabulary

seaweed: a plant that grows in the ocean

tide: the level of the ocean. The tide goes in and out every twelve hours.

Share your answers.

1. Are there any beaches near your home?

2. Do you prefer to spend more time on the sand or in the water?

3. Where are some of the world's best beaches?

A. **walk**
تمشي

B. **jog**
يعدو ببطء

C. **run**
تركض

D. **throw**
يقذف

E. **catch**
يلتقط

F. **pitch**
يرمي

G. **hit**
يضرب

H. **pass**
يمرر

I. **shoot**
يقذف الكرة نحو الهدف

J. **jump**
يقفز

K. **dribble / bounce**
ينطنط الكرة

L. **kick**
يشوط

M. **tackle**
يمسك بالخصم لإيقافه

Practice talking about what you can do.

I can <u>swim</u>, but I can't <u>dive</u>.

I can <u>pass the ball</u> well, but I can't <u>shoot</u> too well.

Use the new language.

Look at **Individual Sports**, page **159**.

Name the actions you see people doing.

The man in number 18 is riding a horse.

N. serve
يستهل ضرب الكرة

O. swing
يوجِه

P. exercise / work out
يتدرب

Q. stretch
يتمدد

R. bend
ينحني

S. dive
يغوص

T. swim
يسبح

U. ski
يتزلَج على الثلج

V. skate
يتزلج

W. ride
يركب

X. start
ينطلق

Y. race
يسابق

Z. finish
يصل لخط النهاية

Share your answers.
1. What do you like to do?
2. What do you have difficulty doing?
3. How often do you exercise? Once a week? Two or three times a week? More? Never?
4. Which is more difficult, throwing a ball or catching it?

1. score
نتيجة الاصابات في اللعبة
2. coach
مدرّب
3. team
فريق
4. fan
مؤيد
5. player
لاعب
6. official/referee
حكم
7. basketball court
ملعب كرة سلة

8. basketball
كرة السلة
9. baseball
بيسبول
10. softball
صوفتبول
11. football
فوتبول أمريكي
12. soccer
كرة القدم
13. ice hockey
لعبة الهوكي
14. volleyball
الكرة الطائرة
15. water polo
كرة الماء

More vocabulary

captain: the team leader

umpire: in baseball, the name for the referee

Little League: a baseball league for children

win: to have the best score

lose: the opposite of win

tie: to have the same score as the other team

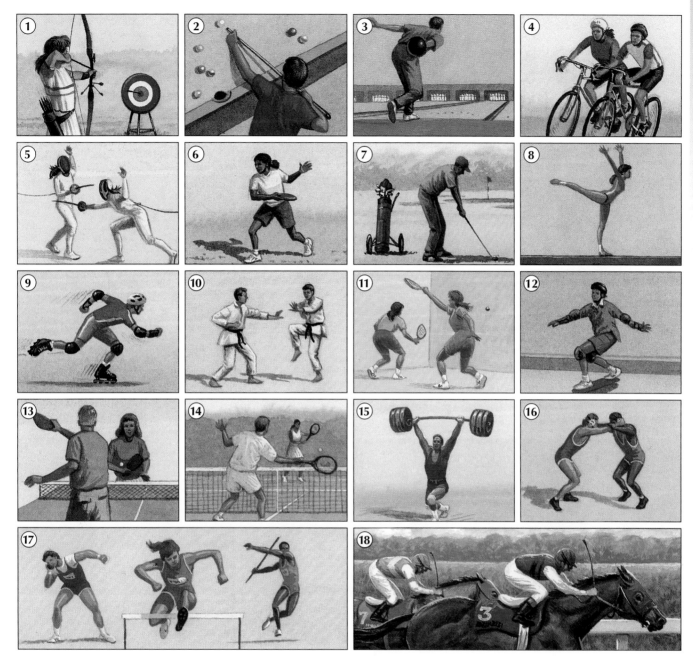

1. archery
رماية السهام

2. billiards/pool
بلیارد

3. bowling
بولنغ

4. cycling/biking
ركوب الدراجة

5. fencing
مبارزة بالسيف

6. flying disc*
القرص الطائر

7. golf
الجولف

8. gymnastics
الرياضة الجمبازية

9. inline skating
التزلج بمزلجة دواليب

10. martial arts
الجودو

11. racquetball
الراكتبول

12. skateboarding
التزلج على لوح بعجلات

13. table tennis/
Ping-Pong™
كرة الطاولة

14. tennis
كرة المضرب

15. weightlifting
رفع الأثقال

16. wrestling
المصارعة

17. track and field
سباق المضمار والميدان

18. horse racing
سباق الخيول

*Note: one brand is Frisbee®
(Mattel, Inc.)

Talk about sports.

Which sports do you like?

   I like <u>tennis</u> but I don't like <u>golf</u>.

Share your answers.

1. Which sports are good for children to learn? Why?

2. Which sport is the most difficult to learn? Why?

3. Which sport is the most dangerous? Why?

1. downhill skiing
التزلج على منحدر

2. snowboarding
التزلج على الثلج

3. cross-country skiing
التزلج في الضاحية

4. ice skating
التزلج على الجليد

5. figure skating
التزلج مع القيام بسلسلة حركات

6. sledding
ركوب المزلجة

7. waterskiing
التزلج على الماء

8. sailing
الابحار بمركب شراعي

9. surfing
ركوب الأمواج المتكسرة

10. sailboarding
الابحار والتزلج

11. snorkeling
السباحة مع استعمال أنبوب التنفس

12. scuba diving
الغوص مع خزان التنفس

Use the new language.

Look at **The Beach**, page **155**.

Name the sports you see.

Share your answers.

1. Which sports are in the Winter Olympics?

2. Which sports do you think are the most exciting to watch?

1. golf club هراوة جولف	**8.** target هدف	**15.** catcher's mask قناع ممسك الكرة	**22.** football كرة فوتبول أمريكي
2. tennis racket مضرب كرة التنس	**9.** ice skates مزلج جليد	**16.** uniform زي موحّد	**23.** snowboard لوحة للتزلج على الثلج
3. volleyball كرة الطائرة	**10.** inline skates مزلج بخط دواليب	**17.** glove قفاز	**24.** skis مزلجة
4. basketball كرة السلة	**11.** hockey stick عصا هوكي	**18.** baseball بيسبول	**25.** ski poles عصا تزلج
5. bowling ball كرة البولنغ	**12.** soccer ball كرة قدم	**19.** weights أثقال	**26.** ski boots حذاء تزلج
6. bow قوس	**13.** shin guards واقيات قصبة الرجل	**20.** football helmet خوذة فوتبول أمريكي	**27.** flying disc* قرص طائر
7. arrow سهم	**14.** baseball bat مضرب بيسبول	**21.** shoulder pads لبادة كتف	***Note:** one brand is Frisbee® (Mattel, Inc.)

Share your answers.

1. Which sports equipment is used for safety reasons?

2. Which sports equipment is heavy?

3. What sports equipment do you have at home?

Use the new language.

Look at **Individual Sports,** page **159.**

Name the sports equipment you see.

Hobbies and Games   هوايات وألعاب

A. collect things	**B. play** games	**C. build** models	**D. do** crafts
تجمع أشياء	يلعب ألعاب	تبني نماذج	يقوم بأعمال يدوية

1. video game system
جهاز لألعاب الفيديو

2. cartridge
خرطوشة

3. board game
لعبة لوحية

4. dice
زهر الطاولة/ النرد

5. checkers
رقعة الداما

6. chess
شطرنج

7. model kit
عدة لتركيب نماذج

8. glue
صمغ

9. acrylic paint
دهان أكريليك

10. figurine
تمثال صغير

11. baseball card
بطاقة بيسبول

12. stamp collection
جمع الطوابع

13. coin collection
جمع العملات النقدية

14. clay
عجينة طين

15. doll making kit
مجموعة لعمل الدمي

16. woodworking kit
عدّة النجارة

Talk about how much time you spend on your hobbies.

I _do crafts_ all the time.

I _play chess_ sometimes.

I never _build models_.

Share your answers.

1. How often do you play video games? Often? Sometimes? Never?

2. What board games do you know?

3. Do you collect anything? What?

E. paint	**F. knit**	**G. pretend**	**H. play** cards
ترسم بالأصباغ	تحبك بالصنارة	تتظاهر	يعلب ورق الشدة

17. yarn	**21. easel**	**25. watercolor**	**29. hearts**
لفيفة صوف/ قطن	حامل لوح	ألوان مائية	الكوبة
18. knitting needles	**22. canvas**	**26. clubs**	**30. paper doll**
أسياخ حياكة	قماش قنب	الاسباتي	لعبة من ورق
19. embroidery	**23. paintbrush**	**27. diamonds**	**31. action figure**
تطريز	فرشاة قنب	الديناري	تماثيل أبطال
20. crochet	**24. oil paint**	**28. spades**	**32. model trains**
حبك بصنارة معقوفة	فرشاة رسم	البستوني	قطارات لعب نموذجية

Share your answers.

1. Do you like to play cards? Which games?

2. Did you pretend a lot when you were a child? What did you pretend to be?

3. Is it important to have hobbies? Why or why not?

4. What's your favorite game?

5. What's your hobby?

1. clock radio
راديو بساعة

2. portable radio-cassette player
آلة كاسيت نقالة

3. cassette recorder
آلة تسجيل كاسيت

4. microphone
ميكروفون

5. shortwave radio
راديو موجات قصيرة

6. TV (television)
تلفزيون

7. portable TV
تلفزيون نقال

8. VCR (videocassette recorder)
جهاز تسجيل فيديو

9. remote control
جهاز تحكم عن بعد

10. videocassette
كاسيت فيديو

11. speakers
سماعات ستيريو

12. turntable
جهاز تشغيل اسطوانات

13. tuner
جهاز توليف

14. CD player
جهاز تشغيل سي دي

15. personal radio-cassette player
جهاز راديو وكاسيت شخصي

16. headphones
سماعات رأس

17. adapter
مهايئ

18. plug
قابس

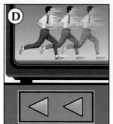
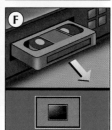

19. video camera
آلة فيديو

20. tripod
حامل ثلاثي القوائم

21. camcorder
آلة تسجيل فيديو

22. battery pack
حزمة بطاريات

23. battery charger
شاحن بطاريات

24. 35 mm camera
كاميرا

25. zoom lens
عدسة تزويم

26. film
فيلم

27. camera case
حقيبة آلة تصوير

28. screen
شاشة

29. carousel slide projector
جهاز عرض دوار للسلايدز

30. slide tray
حامل السلايدز

31. slides
سلايدز

32. photo album
ألبوم صور

33. out of focus
صورة غير واضحة

34. overexposed
صورة زائدة التعريض للضوء

35. underexposed
صورة ناقصة التعريض للضوء

A. record
يسجّل

B. play
يشغل

C. fast forward
يقدّم الصورة بسرعة

D. rewind
يَرجع الشريط

E. pause
يوقف مؤقتا

F. stop and **eject**
يوقف ويُخرج الشريط

Types of entertainment أنواع الوسائل الترفيهية

1. film/movie
فيلم سينمائي

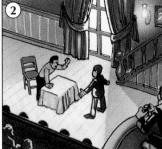

2. play
مسرحية

3. television program
برنامج تلفزيوني

4. radio program
برنامج إذاعي

5. stand-up comedy
ممثل هزلي أمام الجمهور

6. concert
حفلة موسيقية

7. ballet
رقص البالية

8. opera
الأوبرا، مسرحية موسيقية

Types of stories أنواع القصص

9. western
فلم رعاة البقر

10. comedy
مسرحية هزلية

11. tragedy
تراجيديا

12. science fiction story
رواية خيالية

13. action story/
adventure story
رواية مغامرات

14. horror story
رواية مرعبة

15. mystery
رواية بوليسية

16. romance
رواية حب

Types of TV programs أنواع البرامج التلفزيونية

17. news
الأخبار

18. sitcom (situation comedy)
برنامج تلفزيوني (كوميديا)

19. cartoon
أفلام كرتون

20. talk show
مقابلات

21. soap opera
مسلسل دراما

22. nature program
برنامج عن الطبيعة

23. game show/quiz show
منافسة أو مسابقة

24. children's program
برنامج أطفال

25. shopping program
برنامج بيع

26. serious book
كتاب جدّي

27. funny book
كتاب مضحك

28. sad book
كتاب محزن

29. boring book
كتاب ممل

30. interesting book
كتاب مثير للاهتمام

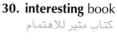

167

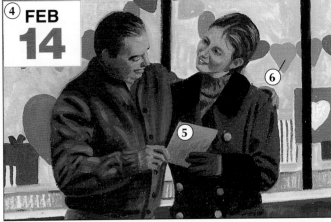

1. New Year's Day
يوم رأس السنة

2. parade
موكب استعراضي

3. confetti
قصاصات النثار الورقية

4. Valentine's Day
عيد الحب

5. card
بطاقة

6. heart
قلب

7. Independence Day/4th of July
عيد الاستقلال/ ٤ يوليو (آب)

8. fireworks
ألعاب نارية

9. flag
راية

10. Halloween
عيد التنكِر

11. jack-o'-lantern
مصباح يصنع من قرعة

12. mask
قناع

13. costume
لباس تنكري

14. candy
حلوى

15. Thanksgiving
عيد الشكر

16. feast
وليمة

17. turkey
ديك رومي

18. Christmas
عيد الميلاد

19. ornament
زينة

20. Christmas tree
شجرة عيد الميلاد

A. **plan** a party
يعتزم/ تعتزم لحفلة

B. **invite** the guests
يدعو/ تدعو الضيوف

C. **decorate** the house
يزين المنزل

D. **wrap** a gift
يلف/ تلف هدية

E. **hide**
يختبئ/ تختبئ

F. **answer** the door
يرد/ ترد على الباب

G. **shout** "surprise!"
يصيح/ تصيح «مفاجأة»

H. **light** the candles
تشعل الشمعات

I. **sing** "Happy Birthday"
يغني/ تغني «سنة حلوة»

J. **make** a wish
تتمنى

K. **blow out** the candles
تطفئ الشمعات

L. **open** the presents
تفتح الهدايا

Practice inviting friends to a party.

I'd love for you to come to my party <u>next week</u>.

Could <u>you and your friend</u> come to my party?

Would <u>your friend</u> like to come to a party I'm giving?

Share your answers.

1. Do you celebrate birthdays? What do you do?

2. Are there birthdays you celebrate in a special way?

3. Is there a special birthday song in your country?

Verb Guide

Verbs in English are either regular or irregular in the past tense and past participle forms.

Regular Verbs

The regular verbs below are marked 1, 2, 3, or 4 according to four different spelling patterns. (See page 172 for the **irregular verbs** which do not follow any of these patterns.)

Spelling Patterns for the Past and the Past Participle	*Example*		
1. Add **-ed** to the end of the verb.	**ASK**	→	**ASKED**
2. Add **-d** to the end of the verb.	**LIVE**	→	**LIVED**
3. Double the final consonant and add **-ed** to the end of the verb.	**DROP**	→	**DROPPED**
4. Drop the final y and add **-ied** to the end of the verb.	**CRY**	→	**CRIED**

The Oxford Picture Dictionary List of Regular Verbs

act (1)
add (1)
address (1)
answer (1)
apologize (2)
appear (1)
applaud (1)
arrange (2)
arrest (1)
arrive (2)
ask (1)
assemble (2)
assist (1)
bake (2)
barbecue (2)
bathe (2)
board (1)
boil (1)
borrow (1)
bounce (2)
brainstorm (1)
breathe (2)
broil (1)
brush (1)
burn (1)
call (1)
carry (4)
change (2)
check (1)
choke (2)
chop (3)
circle (2)
claim (1)
clap (3)
clean (1)
clear (1)
climb (1)
close (2)
collate (2)

collect (1)
color (1)
comb (1)
commit (3)
compliment (1)
conserve (2)
convert (1)
cook (1)
copy (4)
correct (1)
cough (1)
count (1)
cross (1)
cry (4)
dance (2)
design (1)
deposit (1)
deliver (1)
dial (1)
dictate (2)
die (2)
discuss (1)
dive (2)
dress (1)
dribble (2)
drill (1)
drop (3)
drown (1)
dry (4)
dust (1)
dye (2)
edit (1)
eject (1)
empty (4)
end (1)
enter (1)
erase (2)
examine (2)
exchange (2)

exercise (2)
experience (2)
exterminate (2)
fasten (1)
fax (1)
file (2)
fill (1)
finish (1)
fix (1)
floss (1)
fold (1)
fry (4)
gargle (2)
graduate (2)
grate (2)
grease (2)
greet (1)
grill (1)
hail (1)
hammer (1)
harvest (1)
help (1)
hire (2)
hug (3)
immigrate (2)
inquire (2)
insert (1)
introduce (2)
invite (2)
iron (1)
jog (3)
join (1)
jump (1)
kick (1)
kiss (1)
knit (3)
land (1)
laugh (1)
learn (1)

lengthen (1)
listen (1)
live (2)
load (1)
lock (1)
look (1)
mail (1)
manufacture (2)
mark (1)
match (1)
measure (2)
milk (1)
miss (1)
mix (1)
mop (3)
move (2)
mow (1)
need (1)
nurse (2)
obey (1)
observe (2)
open (1)
operate (2)
order (1)
overdose (2)
paint (1)
park (1)
pass (1)
pause (2)
peel (1)
perm (1)
pick (1)
pitch (1)
plan (3)
plant (1)
play (1)
point (1)
polish (1)
pour (1)
pretend (1)
print (1)
protect (1)

pull (1)
push (1)
race (2)
raise (2)
rake (2)
receive (2)
record (1)
recycle (2)
register (1)
relax (1)
remove (2)
rent (1)
repair (1)
repeat (1)
report (1)
request (1)
return (1)
rinse (2)
roast (1)
rock (1)
sauté (2)
save (2)
scrub (3)
seat (1)
sentence (2)
serve (2)
share (2)
shave (2)
ship (3)
shop (3)
shorten (1)
shout (1)
sign (1)
simmer (1)
skate (2)
ski (1)
slice (2)
smell (1)
sneeze (2)
sort (1)
spell (1)
staple (2)

start (1)
stay (1)
steam (1)
stir (3)
stir-fry (4)
stop (3)
stow (1)
stretch (1)
supervise (2)
swallow (1)
tackle (2)
talk (1)
taste (2)
thank (1)
tie (2)
touch (1)
transcribe (2)
transfer (3)
travel (1)
trim (3)
turn (1)
type (2)
underline (2)
unload (1)
unpack (1)
use (2)
vacuum (1)
vomit (1)
vote (2)
wait (1)
walk (1)
wash (1)
watch (1)
water (1)
weed (1)
weigh (1)
wipe (2)
work (1)
wrap (3)
yield (1)

Verb Guide

Irregular Verbs

These verbs have irregular endings in the past and/or the past participle.

The Oxford Picture Dictionary List of Irregular Verbs

simple	past	past participle	simple	past	past participle
be	was	been	leave	left	left
beat	beat	beaten	lend	lent	lent
become	became	become	let	let	let
begin	began	begun	light	lit	lit
bend	bent	bent	make	made	made
bleed	bled	bled	pay	paid	paid
blow	blew	blown	picnic	picnicked	picnicked
break	broke	broken	put	put	put
build	built	built	read	read	read
buy	bought	bought	rewind	rewound	rewound
catch	caught	caught	rewrite	rewrote	rewritten
come	came	come	ride	rode	ridden
cut	cut	cut	run	ran	run
do	did	done	say	said	said
draw	drew	drawn	see	saw	seen
drink	drank	drunk	sell	sold	sold
drive	drove	driven	send	sent	sent
eat	ate	eaten	set	set	set
fall	fell	fallen	sew	sewed	sewn
feed	fed	fed	shoot	shot	shot
feel	felt	felt	sing	sang	sung
find	found	found	sit	sat	sat
fly	flew	flown	speak	spoke	spoken
get	got	gotten	stand	stood	stood
give	gave	given	sweep	swept	swept
go	went	gone	swim	swam	swum
hang	hung	hung	swing	swung	swung
have	had	had	take	took	taken
hear	heard	heard	teach	taught	taught
hide	hid	hidden	throw	threw	thrown
hit	hit	hit	wake	woke	woken
hold	held	held	wear	wore	worn
keep	kept	kept	withdraw	withdrew	withdrawn
lay	laid	laid	write	wrote	written

Index

Two numbers are shown after words in the index: the first refers to the page where the word is illustrated and the second refers to the item number of the word on that page. For example, cool [kōol] **10**-3 means that the word *cool* is item number 3 on page 10. If only the bold page number appears, then that word is part of the unit title or subtitle, or is found somewhere else on the page. A bold number followed by ✦ means the word can be found in the exercise space at the bottom of that page.

Words or combinations of words that appear in **bold** type are used as verbs or verb phrases. Words used as other parts of speech are shown in ordinary type. So, for example, **file** (in bold type) is the verb *file*, while file (in ordinary type) is the noun *file*. Words or phrases in small capital letters (for example, HOLIDAYS) form unit titles.

Phrases and other words that form combinations with an individual word entry are often listed underneath it. Rather than repeating the word each time it occurs in combination with what is listed under it, the word is replaced by three dots (...), called an ellipsis. For example, under the word *bus*, you will find ...driver and ...stop meaning *bus driver* and *bus stop*. Under the word *store* you will find shoe... and toy..., meaning *shoe store* and *toy store*.

Pronunciation Guide

The index includes a pronunciation guide for all the words and phrases illustrated in the book. This guide uses symbols commonly found in dictionaries for native speakers. These symbols, unlike those used in pronunciation systems such as the International Phonetic Alphabet, tend to use English spelling patterns and so should help you to become more aware of the connections between written English and spoken English.

Consonants

[b] as in back [băk]	[k] as in key [kē]	[sh] as in shoe [shōo]
[ch] as in cheek [chēk]	[l] as in leaf [lēf]	[t] as in tape [tāp]
[d] as in date [dāt]	[m] as in match [măch]	[th] as in three [thrē]
[dh] as in this [dhĭs]	[n] as in neck [nĕk]	[v] as in vine [vīn]
[f] as in face [fās]	[ng] as in ring [rĭng]	[w] as in wait [wāt]
[g] as in gas [găs]	[p] as in park [pärk]	[y] as in yams [yămz]
[h] as in half [hăf]	[r] as in rice [rīs]	[z] as in zoo [zōo]
[j] as in jam [jăm]	[s] as in sand [sănd]	[zh] as in measure [mĕzh/ər]

Vowels

[ā] as in bake [bāk]	[ĭ] as in lip [lĭp]	[ow] as in cow [kow]
[ă] as in back [băk]	[ï] as in near [nïr]	[oy] as in boy [boy]
[ä] as in car [kär] or box [bäks]	[ō] as in cold [kōld]	[ŭ] as in cut [kŭt]
[ē] as in beat [bēt]	[ö] as in short [shört]	[ü] as in curb [kürb]
[ĕ] as in bed [bĕd]	or claw [klö]	[ə] as in above [ə bŭv/]
[ë] as in bear [bër]	[ōo] as in cool [kōol]	
[ī] as in line [līn]	[ŏo] as in cook [kŏok]	

All the pronunciation symbols used are alphabetical except for the schwa [ə]. The schwa is the most frequent vowel sound in English. If you use the schwa appropriately in unstressed syllables, your pronunciation will sound more natural.

Vowels before [r] are shown with the symbol [¨] to call attention to the special quality that vowels have before [r]. (Note that the symbols [ä] and [ö] are also used for vowels not followed by [r], as in *box* or *claw*.) You should listen carefully to native speakers to discover how these vowels actually sound.

Stress

This index follows the system for marking stress used in many dictionaries for native speakers.

1. Stress is not marked if a word consisting of a single syllable occurs by itself.

2. Where stress is marked, two levels are distinguished:

a bold accent [/] is placed after each syllable with primary (or strong) stress, a light accent [/] is placed after each syllable with secondary (or weaker) stress.

In phrases and other combinations of words, stress is indicated for each word as it would be pronounced within the whole phrase or other unit. If a word consisting of a single syllable is stressed in the combinations listed below it, the accent mark indicating the degree of stress it has in the phrases (primary or secondary) is shown in parentheses. A hyphen replaces any part of a word or phrase that is omitted. For example, bus [bŭs(/–)] shows that the word *bus* is said with primary stress in the combinations shown below it. The word ...driver [–drī/vər], listed under *bus*, shows that *driver* has secondary stress in the combination *bus driver*: [bŭs/ drī/vər]

Syllable Boundaries

Syllable boundaries are indicated by a single space or by a stress mark.

Note: The pronunciations shown in this index are based on patterns of American English. There has been no attempt to represent all of the varieties of American English. Students should listen to native speakers to hear how the language actually sounds in a particular region.

Index

Index

Index

Index

Index

Index

Index

Index

Index

Index

Index

Index

Geographical Index

Continents

Countries and other locations

Mongolia [mäng gō/lē ə] **124–125**
Montenegro [män/tə nē/grō, –nĕ/–] **124–125**
Morocco [mə räk/ō] **124–125**
Mozambique [mō/zəm bēk/] **124–125**
Myanmar [myän/mär] **124–125**
Namibia [nə mĭb/ē ə] **124–125**
Nauru [nä o͞o/ro͞o] **124–125**
Nepal [nə pöl/, –päl/] **124–125**
Netherlands [nĕdh/ər ləndz] **124–125**
New Guinea [no͞o/ gĭn/ē] **124–125**
New Zealand [no͞o/ zē/lənd] **124–125**
Nicaragua [nĭk/ə rä/gwə] **122–125**
Niger [nī/jər, nē zhër/] **124–125**
Nigeria [nī jïr/ē ə] **124–125**
North Korea [nörth/ kə rē/ə] **124–125**
Norway [nör/wā] **124–125**
Oman [ō män/] **124–125**
Pakistan [păk/ə stän/] **124–125**
Palau [pə low/] **124–125**
Panama [păn/ə mä/] **122–125**
Papua New Guinea [păp/yo͞o ə no͞o/ gĭn/ē] **124–125**
Paraguay [păr/ə gwī/, –gwā/] **124–125**
Peru [pə ro͞o/] **124–125**
Philippines [fĭl/ə pēnz/, fĭl/ə pēnz/] **124–125**
Poland [pō/lənd] **124–125**
Portugal [pör/chə gəl] **124–125**
Puerto Rico [pwër/tə rē/kō, pör/tə–] **122–125**
Qatar [kä/tär, kə tär/] **124–125**
Romania [rō mā/nē ə, ro͞o–] **124–125**
Russia [rŭsh/ə] **124–125**
Rwanda [ro͞o än/də] **124–125**
Saudi Arabia [sow/dē ə rā/bē ə, sö/dē–] **124–125**
Senegal [sĕn/ə göl/, –gäl/] **124–125**
Serbia [sür/bē ə] **124–125**
Seychelles [sā shĕlz/, –shĕl/] **124–125**
Sierra Leone [sē ĕr/ə lē ōn/, –lē ō/nē] **124–125**
Singapore [sĭng/ə pör/] **124–125**
Slovakia [slō vä/kē ə] **124–125**
Slovenia [slō vē/nē ə] **124–125**
Solomon Islands [säl/ə mən ī/ləndz] **124–125**
Somalia [sə mä/lē ə] **124–125**
South Africa [sowth/ ăf/rĭ kə] **124–125**
South Korea [sowth/ kə rē/ə] **124–125**
Spain [spān] **124–125**
Sri Lanka [srē/ läng/kə, shrē/–] **124–125**
Sudan [so͞o dän/] **124–125**
Sumatra [so͞o mä/trə] **124–125**
Suriname [so͞or/ə nä/mə] **124–125**
Swaziland [swä/zē länd/] **124–125**
Sweden [swēd/n] **124–125**
Switzerland [swĭt/sər lənd] **124–125**
Syria [sïr/ē ə] **124–125**
Tahiti [tə hē/tē] **124–125**
Taiwan [tī/wän/] **124–125**
Tajikistan [tä jĭk/ə stän/, –stän/] **124–125**
Tanzania [tăn/zə nē/ə] **124–125**
Tasmania [tăz mā/nē ə] **124–125**
Thailand [tī/lănd/, –lənd] **124–125**
The Gambia [dhə găm/bē ə] **124–125**
Togo [tō/gō] **124–125**
Tonga [täng/gə] **124–125**
Tunisia [to͞o nē/zhə] **124–125**
Turkey [tür/kē] **124–125**
Turkmenistan [türk mĕn/ə stän/, –stän/] **124–125**
Uganda [yo͞o găn/də] **124–125**

Ukraine [yo͞o/krān, yo͞o krān/] **124–125**
United Arab Emirates [yo͞o nī/təd ăr/əb ĕm/ər əts] **124–125**
United Kingdom [yo͞o nī/təd kĭng/dəm] **124–125**
United States of America [yo͞o nī/təd stäts/ əv ə mĕr/ə kə] **122–125**
Uruguay [yo͞or/ə gwī/, –gwā/] **124–125**
Uzbekistan [o͞oz bĕk/ə stän/, –stän/] **124–125**
Venezuela [vĕn/ə zwā/lə] **124–125**
Vietnam [vē/ĕt näm/, –năm/] **124–125**
Western Sahara [wĕs/tərn sə här/ə] **124–125**
Western Samoa [wĕs/tərn sə mō/ə] **124–125**
Yemen [yĕm/ən] **124–125**
Zambia [zăm/bē ə] **124–125**
Zimbabwe [zĭm bäb/wā] **124–125**

Bodies of water
Arabian Sea [ə rā/bē ən sē/] **124–125**
Arctic Ocean [ärk/tĭk ō/shən] **122–125**
Baffin Bay [băf/ən bā/] **122–125**
Baltic Sea [böl/tĭk sē/] **124–125**
Barents Sea [băr/ənts sē/] **124–125**
Beaufort Sea [bō/fərt sē/] **122–125**
Bering Sea [bĕr/ĭng sē/, bïr/–] **122–125**
Black Sea [blăk/ sē/] **124–125**
Caribbean Sea [kăr/ə bē/ən sē/, kə rĭb/ē ən–] **122–125**
Caspian Sea [kăs/pē ən sē/] **124–125**
Coral Sea [kör/əl sē/] **124–125**
East China Sea [ēst/ chī/nə sē/] **124–125**
Greenland Sea [grēn/lənd sē/, –lănd/–] **124–125**
Gulf of Alaska [gŭlf/ əv ə lăs/kə] **122–125**
Gulf of California [gŭlf/ əv kăl/ə förn/yə] **122–125**
Gulf of Honduras [gŭlf/ əv hän do͞or/əs] **122–125**
Gulf of Mexico [gŭlf/ əv mĕk/sĭ kō/] **122–125**
Gulf of St. Lawrence [gŭlf/ əv sānt/ lör/əns, –lär/–] **122–125**
Hudson Bay [hŭd/sən bā/] **122–125**
Indian Ocean [ĭn/dē ən ō/shən] **124–125**
Labrador Sea [lăb/rə dör/ sē/] **122–125**
Mediterranean Sea [mĕd/ə tə rā/nē ən sē/] **124–125**
North Atlantic Ocean [nörth/ ət lăn/tĭk ō/shən] **122–125**
North Pacific Ocean [nörth/ pə sĭf/ĭk ō/shən] **122–125**
North Sea [nörth/ sē/] **124–125**
Norwegian Sea [nör wē/jən sē/] **124–125**
Persian Gulf [pür/zhən gŭlf/] **124–125**
Philippine Sea [fĭl/ə pēn/ sē/] **124–125**
Red Sea [rĕd/ sē/] **124–125**
Sea of Japan [sē/ əv jə pän/] **124–125**
Sea of Okhotsk [sē/ əv ō kätsk/] **124–125**
South Atlantic Ocean [sowth/ ət lăn/tĭk ō/shən] **124–125**
South China Sea [sowth/ chī/nə sē/] **124–125**
Southern Ocean [sŭdh/ərn ō/shən] **124–125**
South Pacific Ocean [sowth/ pə sĭf/ĭk ō/shən] **124–125**

The United States of America
Capital: Washington, D.C. (District Of Columbia)
[wä/shĭng tən dē/sē/, wö/–]

Regions of the United States

States of the United States
Alabama [ăl/ə băm/ə] **122–123**
Alaska [ə lăs/kə] **122–125**
Arizona [ăr/ə zō/nə] **122–123**
Arkansas [är/kən sö/] **122–123**
California [kăl/ə förn/yə] **122–123**
Colorado [kăl/ə răd/ō, –ra/dō] **122–123**
Connecticut [kə nĕt/ĭ kət] **122–123**
Delaware [dĕl/ə wër/] **122–123**
Florida [flör/ə də, flär/–] **122–123**
Georgia [jör/jə] **122–123**
Hawaii [hə wī/ē] **122–123**
Idaho [ī/də hō/] **122–123**
Illinois [ĭl/ə noy/] **122–123**
Indiana [ĭn/dē ăn/ə] **122–123**
Iowa [ī/ə wə] **122–123**
Kansas [kăn/zəs] **122–123**
Kentucky [kən tŭk/ē] **122–123**
Louisiana [loo ē/zē ăn/ə] **122–123**
Maine [mān] **122–123**
Maryland [mër/ə lənd] **122–123**
Massachusetts [măs/ə choo/səts] **122–123**
Michigan [mĭsh/ĭ gən] **122–123**
Minnesota [mĭn/ə sō/tə] **122–123**
Mississippi [mĭs/ə sĭp/ē] **122–123**
Missouri [mə zoor/ē, –zoor/ə] **122–123**
Montana [măn tăn/ə] **122–123**
Nebraska [nə brăs/kə] **122–123**
Nevada [nə văd/ə, –vä/də] **122–123**
New Hampshire [noo/ hămp/shər] **122–123**
New Jersey [noo/ jür/zē] **122–123**
New Mexico [noo/ mĕk/sĭ kō/] **122–123**
New York [noo/ yörk/] **122–123**
North Carolina [nörth/ kăr/ə lī/nə] **122–123**
North Dakota [nörth/ də kō/tə] **122–123**
Ohio [ō hī/ō] **122–123**
Oklahoma [ō/klə hō/mə] **122–123**
Oregon [ör/ĭ gən, –gän/, är/–] **122–123**
Pennsylvania [pĕn/səl vān/yə] **122–123**
Rhode Island [rōd/ ī/lənd] **122–123**
South Carolina [sowth/ kăr/ə lī/nə] **122–123**
South Dakota [sowth/ də kō/tə] **122–123**
Tennessee [tĕn/ə sē/] **122–123**
Texas [tĕk/səs] **122–123**
Utah [yoo/tö, –tä] **122–123**
Vermont [vər mänt/] **122–123**
Virginia [vər jĭn/yə] **122–123**
Washington [wä/shĭng tən, wö/–] **122–123**
West Virginia [wĕst/ vər jĭn/yə] **122–123**
Wisconsin [wĭs kän/sən] **122–123**
Wyoming [wī ō/mĭng] **122–123**

Canada
Capital: Ottawa [ät/ə wə]

Regions of Canada
Atlantic Provinces [ət lăn/tĭk präv/ən səz] **123–6**
British Columbia [brĭt/ĭsh kə lŭm/bē ə] **123–2**
Northern Canada [nör/dhərn kăn/ə də] **123–1**
Ontario [än tër/ē ō/] **123–4**
Prairie Provinces [prë/ē präv/ən səz] **123–3**
Quebec [kwĭ bĕk/] **123–5**

Provinces of Canada
Alberta [ăl bür/tə] **122–123**
British Columbia [brĭt/ĭsh kə lŭm/bē ə] **122–123**
Manitoba [măn/ə tō/bə] **122–123**

New Brunswick [noo/ brŭnz/wĭk] **122–123**
Newfoundland [noo/fən lənd] **122–123**
Northwest Territories [nörth/wĕst/ tĕr/ə tör/ēz] **122–123**
Nova Scotia [nō/və skō/shə] **122–123**
Ontario [än tër/ē ō/] **122–123**
Prince Edward Island [prĭns/ ĕd/wərd ī/lənd] **122–123**
Quebec [kwĭ bĕk/] **122–123**
Saskatchewan [să skăch/ə wən, –wän/] **122–123**
Yukon Territory [yoo/kän tĕr/ə tör/ē] **122–123**

Mexico
Capital: Mexico (City) [mĕk/sĭ kō/ (sĭt/ē)]

Regions of Mexico
Chiapas Highlands [chē ä/pəs hī/ləndz] **123–18**
Gulf Coastal Plain [gŭlf/ kō/stəl plān/] **123–16**
Pacific Northwest [pə sĭf/ĭk nörth/wĕst] **123–14**
Plateau of Mexico [plă tō/ əv mĕk/sĭ kō/] **123–15**
Southern Uplands [sŭdh/ərn ŭp/ləndz] **123–17**
Yucatan Peninsula [yoo/kə tăn/ pə nĭn/sə lə, yoo/kə tän/–] **123–19**

States of Mexico
Aguascalientes [ä/gwəs käl yĕn/tās] **122–123**
Baja California Norte [bä/hä kăl/ə förn/yə nör/tä] **122–123**
Baja California Sur [bä/hä kăl/ə förn/yə soor/] **122–123**
Campeche [käm pā/chä, käm pē/chē] **122–123**
Chiapas [chē ä/pəs] **122–123**
Chihuahua [chĭ wä/wä, –wə] **122–123**
Coahuila [kō/ə wē/lə] **122–123**
Colima [kə lē/mə] **122–123**
Distrito Federal [dĭ strē/tō fĕd/ə räl/] **122–123**
Durango [doo räng/gō, –räng/–] **122–123**
Guanajuato [gwä/nə hwä/tō] **122–123**
Guerrero [gə rër/ō] **122–123**
Hidalgo [hĭ däl/gō, ē dhäl/gō] **122–123**
Jalisco [hə lĭs/kō, –lēs/–] **122–123**
México [mĕk/sĭ kō/, mĕ/hē kō] **122–123**
Michoacán [mē/chō ä kän/] **122–123**
Morelos [mö rēl/ōs] **122–123**
Nayarit [nä/yə rēt/] **122–123**
Nuevo León [nwā/vō lā ōn/] **122–123**
Oaxaca [wə hä/kə, wä–] **122–123**
Puebla [pwĕb/lä] **122–123**
Querétaro [kə rēt/ə rō/] **122–123**
Quintana Roo [kēn tä/nə rō/] **122–123**
San Luis Potosí [sän/ loo ēs/ pō/tə sē/] **122–123**
Sinaloa [sē/nə lō/ə] **122–123**
Sonora [sə nör/ə] **122–123**
Tabasco [tə bäs/kō] **122–123**
Tamaulipas [tä/mow lē/pəs] **122–123**
Tlaxcala [tlä skä/lə] **122–123**
Veracruz [vĕr/ə krooz/, –kroos/] **122–123**
Yucatán [yoo/kə tän/, –tän/] **122–123**
Zacatecas [zä/kə tä/kəs, sä/–] **122–123**

ثوب حمام/برنس 67-8	تنورة قصيرة 71-35	**تقاطع طرق 90-91**	**تسلية وترفيه 166-167**
ثوب للرقص 67-1	تنورة مضلعة 65-25	تقرأ الصحيفة V-27	تسمم من مبيدات الحشرات 126-14
سترة يرتديها العمال 65-16	التهاب الحنجرة 78-6	تقرأ قصة F-94	**التسوق 121**
ثوم 51-29	التهاب في الاذن 79-3	تقسيم 118-4	تشاهد التلفزيون S-27
جائع/ـة 30-5	التهاب في الحنجرة 79-4	تُقصّر D-73	تشربت السم J-82
جار 37-22	تهبط/تصل O-111	تقع O-82	تشرف على الموظفين K-140
جاروف 149-21	تهجى اسمك A-4	تقلع/تغادر L-111	تشطف الشعر F-76
جاروف/رفش 39-13	تهجى الكلمة.E-6	تقلم الاظافر N-77	تشعر بالغثيان D-78
جاروف/لقاطة الكناسة 47-11	تهز H-94	تقود سيارة C-90	تشعل الشمعات H-169
جاكيت 66-7	التواء الكاحل 78-18	تقوم على خدمة الزبائن O-140	تصفف الشعر بالفرشاة I-76
جاكيت ثقيل 71-41	التوبة 120-14	**التقويم 18**	تضع الغسيل في الغسالة C-72
جاكيت خفيف 71-40	توت 128-20	تكوي الملابس G-72	تضع حزام الأمان I-111
جاكيت طويل 66-15	توتة العليق 50-18	تلال 117-16	تضع مستحضر حاجز للشمس D-76
جاكيت من الكتان 70-17	تُوسّع F-73	تلبس J-94	تضع المكياج P-77
جالون عصير تفاح 57-5	توصل A-94	تلسكوب 127-21	تضيف مسحوق الغسيل B-72
جامع 89-23	توقع عقد الايجار C-35	تلعب K-94	تُضيّق E-73
جاموس 134-6	توقف/توقفي 107-3	تلفزيون 164-6	تطبع رسالة D-142
الجبر 118-25	توقيت آلاسكا 17-25	تلفزيون نقال 164-7	تطريز 163-19
جبص 81-29	التوقيت الأطلنطي 17-30	تلمع الأثاث K-46	تطعم D-94
جبن 54-38	التوقيت الباسيفيكي 17-26	**تلوث 126**	تطفأ الشمعات K-169
جبن امريكي 53-9	التوقيت الجبلي 17-27	تلويث الجو 126-10	تطلي الاظافر O-77
جبن جاك 53-12	التوقيت الشتوي 17-32	تلويث المياه 126-12	تُطوّل C-73
جبن سويسري 53-11	التوقيت الصيفي 17-33	تليفزيون 42-26	تطوي الملابس F-72
جبن شدر 53-10	توقيت الولايات الشرقية 17-29	تليفون خلوي 9-13	تعالج بالأبر الصينية G-81
جبهة 74-20	توقيت الولايات الوسطى 17-28	تليفون عام 91-21	تعاون بالكتاب I-6
جبيرة لليد 83-11	توقيت نيو فاوند لاند 17-31	تليفون عام 9-11	تُعاير المقادير A-57
الجد 24-3	توقيت هاواي–الوشيان 17-24	تليفون نقال 9-12	تعبر الشارع A-90
جدار داخلي 149-18	التونة (سمك التن) 130-9	تماثيل 152-9	تعتني بالأطفال L-140
الجدة 24-2	تي شرت جاف 72-18	تماثيل أبطال 163-31	تعد الصحف للاستعمال ثانية B-46
الجدّين 24-1	تي شرت مبلل 72-17	تمثال صغير 162-10	تعريفة/أجرة 104-5
جدري الماء 79-6	تي شرت متسخ 72-15	تمر باضطراب جوي N-111	تعطي D-21
جدول 104-3	تي شرت نظيف 72-16	تمزّق 70-23	تعلق الملابس H-72
جذر 129-3	التيار الكهربائي مقطوع 48-2	تمساح 131-36	تعلم السواقة 121-5
جذع 128-4	ثانية 16-1	تمسح الطاولة O-46	تعمل نسخ E-142
جذع 129-4	ثدي 74-14	تمسح الغبار عن الأثاث A-46	تعيّن موعداً A-85
جذور 128-5	**الثدييات 134-135**	تمشط الشعر G-76	تغسل الشعر E-76
جراج سيارات/موقف سيارات 89-26	**الثدييات البحرية 131**	تمشي A-156	تغسل النوافذ D-46
جراد البحر 53-23	ثعلب 134-15	تنتقل الى الشقة D-35	تغص L-82
جرافة لشق الطرق 149-6	ثقب الباب 37-27	تنجب طفلا M-29	تغير الحفاض E-94
جرثومة نقص المناعة البشرية 79-10	ثقابة آلية 149-9	التنزه سيرا على الأقدام 154-6	تغير الملاءات P-46
جرح 78-13	ثلاث مرات في الأسبوع 18-24	تنظر إلى الحنجرة E-85	تفاح 50-4
جرذ (جرذان) 49-27	الثلاثاء 18-3	تنظف الأرض بالفرشاة L-46	التفاضل والتكامل 118-28
جرذ 133-18	ثلاثة أرباع 15-5	تنظف الفرن C-46	تفتح الهدايا L-169
جرّاح 87-30	ثلاجة 40-9	تنظف المنزل N-27	تفجر البركان 103-14
جرس الاستدعاء 86-10	ثُلث 15-3	تنظف مكان تجمّع النسالة D-72	تفحص العينين F-85
جرس الباب 38-10	ثمانون في المائة 15-10	تنفس انقاذ 83-16	تفحص درجة الحرارة C-85
جرو 133-12	ثمر الببايا 50-20	تنفس 64-10	تفحص ضغط الدم B-85
جريمة 100	ثمر العنبة 50-19	تنورة بفتحة 65-25	تُفرز الغسيل A-72
جريمة القتل 100-8	ثُمن 15-1	تنورة طويلة 71-34	تفرغ المحتويات E-35